ANNUAL

Hitchcock

—2010—

T0334927

Sidney Gottlieb and Richard Allen

Editorial Advisory Board
Charles Barr   Lesley Brill
Paula Marantz Cohen   Leonard J. Leff
Thomas M. Leitch   James Naremore

Founding Editor
Christopher Brookhouse

Editorial Assistant
Renata Jackson

Cover Design
Deborah Dutko

The *Hitchcock Annual* is published each spring. Send correspondence and submissions to either Sidney Gottlieb, Department of Communications and Media Studies, Sacred Heart University, Fairfield, CT 06825 or Richard Allen, Department of Cinema Studies, New York University, Tisch School of the Arts, 721 Broadway, 6th floor, New York, NY 10003. E-mail addresses: spgottlieb@aol.com or Richard.Allen@nyu.edu

For all orders, including back issues, contact Columbia University Press, 61 West 62nd Street, New York, NY 10023; www.columbia/edu/cu/cup

We invite articles on all aspects of Hitchcock's life, works, and influence, and encourage a variety of critical approaches, methods, and viewpoints. For all submissions, follow the guidelines of the *Chicago Manual of Style*, using full notes rather than works cited format. If submitting by mail, send two copies (only one of which will be returned) and return postage. But we prefer submissions via e-mail, which makes it easier to circulate essays for editorial review. The responsibility for securing any permissions required for publishing material in the essay rests with the author. Illustrations may be included, but as separate TIFF files rather than as part of the text file. Decision time is normally within three months. The submission of an essay indicates your commitment to publish it, if accepted, in the *Hitchcock Annual*, and that it is not simultaneously under consideration for publication elsewhere.

The *Hitchcock Annual* is indexed in the *Film Literature Index* and *MLA International Bibliography*.

♛ Columbia University Press   New York

Columbia University Press
Publishers Since 1893
New York   Chichester, West Sussex

Copyright © 2010 Sidney Gottlieb/*Hitchcock Annual*
All rights reserved

ISBN 978-0-231-15649-3 (pbk. : alk. paper)
ISSN 1062-5518

∞
Columbia University Press books are printed on
permanent and durable acid-free paper.
This book is printed on paper with recycled content.

Printed in the United States of America

p 10 9 8 7 6 5 4 3 2 1

References to Internet Web sites (URLs) were accurate at the
time of writing. Neither the editors nor Columbia University
Press are responsible for URLs that may have expired or
changed since the manuscript was prepared

.HITCHCOCK ANNUAL
2010

SIDNEY GOTTLIEB

Hitchcock in 1928:
The Auteur as Autocrat

It is interesting to note that Hitchcock's two most detailed biographers highlight late 1927/early 1928 as a time when authoritarian control comes to prominence as a key issue in his life and central part of his conception of himself as a filmmaker. Donald Spoto suggests that with the exception of *Blackmail* (1929) and *Rich and Strange* (1932), Hitchcock's films made at British International Pictures (B.I.P.) between 1928 and 1932 lack the "passion and intensity associated with his later British films and most of his American films," qualities that were, as Hitchcock was painfully aware, difficult to cultivate with only limited power to shape his films.[1] Spoto relates Hitchcock's desire to achieve such power at this time not to "the simple desire of a tyrannical ego to manage everything and everyone as much as he could" (although this would, he says, become a problem in later years "and cause much unhappiness") but to artistic integrity and a well-justified "profound inner conviction that he did indeed know better than others what would work in the formulation and expression of an idea." Frustrated by forced collaborations and studio-imposed assignments, he was at best able to make his "touch . . . everywhere evident," but "it is a "mistake," Spoto says, to assert that there is "a consistent vision to his early work" (121). As some kind of compensation for the fact that he could not direct films the way he wanted to and achieve his "overarching vision of what the final product should be," though, he was at least able to "exert considerable creative control in his personal life . . . over the situations and people he directed in his notorious practical jokes" (122). Spoto fills four pages with the "nasty and demeaning" (124) details of this redirected energy and spleen, and they sketch a portrait of a disappointed and defensive artist closer to the end of his tether than the height of his powers.

Patrick McGilligan's description of Hitchcock at this time is not nearly as dark as Spoto's, but he too gives detailed coverage of Hitchcock's practical joking, which includes some "innocent" stunts but also others based on "one-upmanship— a game Hitchcock was driven to win at all costs" and "bullying."[2] No Freudian analyst was needed, then or now, to understand what was going on: "Everyone knew his jokes were at their worst when a film wasn't going right." But McGilligan puts this behavior in broader contexts not mentioned by Spoto: "Another souvenir Hitchcock brought back from Germany was the playful tyranny in his persona; a tyranny that was very German, mingled with a playfulness that was very much his own" (98). McGilligan notes that "in the late 1920s emerge the first eyewitness accounts of a director who sometimes ruled the set like a führer, manipulating the people and the atmosphere the way he manipulated pieces of film. To get what he wanted on film, he was capable of behaving like a dictator, or a circus clown" (98). This involved all sorts of "odd behavior," including smashing teacups to call his players and technicians back to work and berating "uninvited visitors to the set" with "curses and obscenities" (99) because of their unwanted disruption of the work of a serious artist. Much in contrast with Spoto, McGilligan sees this "odd behavior" as integrated into Hitchcock's working method and directorial persona rather than as primarily a vehicle for frustration and redirected creativity and control: "Such eccentric behavior woke people up," he says, and "The crew relished it, which was sensible policy" (98). And even the practical jokes seem to have positive functions, as appropriate "comeuppances" for stuffy associates and ways of consolidating friendships with trusted co-workers and kindred spirits, like his cameraman, Jack Cox. Overall, McGilligan, unlike Spoto, sees this as a time of triumph for Hitchcock, not only because of frequent high praise in the newspapers and trade journals for his most recent pictures and recognition of him as one of the highlights and saviors of English cinema (98), but also because he seemed to be developing successful strategies for attaining and wielding the kind of authorial control he sought and forging a public persona that made his quest for such power acceptable, even charming.

To these valuable divergent interpretations of Hitchcock's struggle at this time with interrelated issues of personal and artistic control, we can now add additional evidence and another voice, Hitchcock's own, available in a newly uncovered essay he wrote that as far as I can tell has not been cited or commented on since it was published. The essay is titled "An Autocrat of the Film Studio" and it appeared in the January 1928 issue of *Cassell's Magazine*. While pursuing research in the Truffaut archives, Nancy F. and James M. Vest came across a partial copy of the original article and were able to get a complete copy from the British Library, which they very generously sent to me, and which I reprint below, following a few introductory comments.

"An Autocrat of the Film Studio" is Hitchcock's fullest statement, at this or any other time, of his idea of what in another essay published a few months earlier he called "One-Man Pictures." He concludes "Films We Could Make" (1927) with the assertion "that when moving pictures are really artistic they will be created entirely by one man" (167), and these were far from his last words on the subject.[3] Perhaps at this time he was chafing for even more control than he had been granted to that point, and emboldened by his new-found critical and commercial success. The year was by any measure surely a good one for him: in 1927, his first three films, *The Pleasure Garden*, *The Mountain Eagle*, and *The Lodger*, after being temporarily shelved, were released to much acclaim; he directed and released three more, *Downhill*, *Easy Virtue*, and *The Ring*, the last of which was particularly well received; and he completed a fourth, *The Farmer's Wife*, which would be released in early 1928. On a personal note, he and Alma had married a year earlier and by the end of 1927 knew that they were expecting their first child. In the two areas of his life that really mattered to him, Hitchcock faced challenges of settling into his role as successful director and producer, and it is perhaps not surprising that professional details and domestic metaphors are interspersed throughout his published meditation on his new responsibilities and desires.

The headnote to the essay conveys just how successful and respected he was at the time, describing him as "Britain's foremost film director, with a salary already "twice as much as the Prime Minister's," and a contract that called for it to be raised from £10,000 to £15,000 a year "three years hence."[4] And in true Hitchcock fashion, the visuals as much as the words tell the story here: five of the six illustrations for the article show him in command, directing the actors in various films, quite forcefully supervising the action even when pausing for a haircut on the set of *The Ring,* and the remaining photo is a portrait of an intensely serious and imposing figure, a "young man . . . still in his twenties," to be sure, but one who radiates determination and authority.

The essay is as "outspoken and illuminating" as the headnote suggests, and Hitchcock begins with a bold declaration of the independence of film from literature, emphasizing the need for "its entire severance from both the stage and the novel." He immediately specifies that his primary concern is form, not content. A director can presumably get a story from any source—nearly all of Hitchcock's own films up to this point were in fact based on literary works—but the medium of film can only reach "absolute perfection" by becoming "capable of telling a story in its own way." In sketching out an early version of what he would later call "pure cinema," he characteristically stresses the importance of abandoning words for "a series of moving tableaux which tell a story without the aid of titles and captions." He also characteristically identifies himself as one of the pioneers dedicated to this effort, vowing that "for my part I shall do what I can to develop the film along these lines."

Although it is in some respects fundamentally about film theory, the essay is structured around personification and anecdote rather than abstract conceptual analysis, and this makes it particularly dramatic, accessible, and engaging. Hitchcock presents himself as the exemplary and visionary director, beleaguered by a variety of people, representing anti-cinematic forces of one kind or another, who must be endured, resisted, and ultimately educated and transformed. Confronting these individuals and groups gives Hitchcock the opportunity to focus on the prevailing misinformation about filmmaking that must be cleared away before he and the cinema in general can make any real progress. The ignorance of the filmgoing public in particular needs to be addressed. A key section of this public, the "vast congregation of film aspirants," for example, is unaware that "a film director does not select casts for his films" in the way that they "seem to think," and their relentless advice is not only a personal nuisance— "They bombard me mercilessly with letters setting out their remarkable qualifications for making a name on the films"—but proof positive of why filmmaking should be left in more capable hands.

Hitchcock's precise and knowledgeable remarks on what is critical in casting confirm his legitimate authority as a filmmaker and also further define what he considers to be the essential components of cinema. For example, contrary to popular belief, a beautiful face is not nearly as important as one that is "strong" and "expressive." The actors are above all visual elements in a highly articulated formal structure— something that a general audience not yet trained to give "the photoplay the same serious attention that they give to stage plays" would normally fail to recognize. It takes an experienced and thoughtful director to know that the guiding principle should always be "Don't forget the camera in film work," and to cultivate the kind of understanding of films that would make clear the somewhat counterintuitive idea that the spectator is a secondary, although of course by no means negligible, concern: "In this matter of personal appearance it is more a question of correct focus and lights and shades than a pleasing general appearance."

Interestingly, Hitchcock confesses that the archetypal representative of the ignorant audience is "my own mother," the first of a series of familial references and metaphors that are introduced in key places throughout the rest of the essay. Her annoyance at occasionally finding that she "had already seen the films," the result of her "careless and unobservant" habit of "going to the pictures" without even a minimal effort to know exactly what was being shown, pales in comparison to Hitchcock's justifiable distress at such "flippant indifference which makes me very angry at times, more especially because it seems as if the public, my own mother among them, cannot take the film seriously." In using his mother as his primary example, Hitchcock identifies this attitude not only as "a grave fault and an injustice to a work of art and an industry worthy of intelligent support" but also a deeply felt personal betrayal.[5]

The early memories he goes on to relate are thus not ones of nurturance and reliable maternal guidance and support, but of finding his own way as a boy in studying films seriously—which he insists enhances rather than diminishes one's enjoyment of them—and watching plays with an eye toward whether or not they could be adapted cinematically. He grows up quickly in the span of three paragraphs here: in one moment he is a dedicated, intelligent, and "arrogant" youth critically watching Mrs. Belloc Lowndes's "Who is He?" at the Haymarket Theatre, and in the next he is "a man in my twenties" making the necessary adjustments and directing it as an acclaimed film, *The Lodger*, "familiar by now to millions of cinema-goers." He grows up even more as he concludes his reminiscence and lesson by moving beyond anger and impatience to what he clearly frames as a kind of paternal wisdom and tolerance. The film public may be "indifferent" and ignorant, but it is also, much to his astonishment, "by some miracle of sub-conscious understanding" able to "know when a film is good and when another is bad." The director's "business" is to find ways to cultivate "the approval of his critical yet untaught public," pleasing and when possible educating them. A tried and true metaphor conveys these multiple responsibilities: "He is a kind of film father providing for his family. The family know what they like, but are sublimely ignorant of all that has gone to the making of their feast."

One of the first things that the "film father" needs to do is explain that he works in a factory. Hitchcock's statement that a studio is "nothing more than an 'emotion factory'" (interestingly, not the conventional "dream factory") is perhaps an intentional and in any event a telling echo and revision of D.W. Griffith's well-known references to filmmaking as like grinding out sausages. Like Griffith, he emphasizes that the process of creating even a romance is anything but romantic, but he gives a more detailed and complex analysis than Griffith of "how difficult is this business of 'emotion manufacture.'" Fans who typically believe that their ability to feel emotions means that they could easily "portray" them in a film if only they were given the opportunity are doubly mistaken. They underestimate the remarkable skill of actors who do what they do in a factory-like atmosphere "in the presence of a multitude of distractions." But on a more fundamental level, they do not understand that cinematic effects are created not by enacting emotions but by "the combined attack of the director, the artistes and the camera"—to say the least, a strikingly blunt and revealing formulation of the mechanics of film. "Attack" is only one of a cluster of militant metaphors used in this section of the essay that convey not only Hitchcock's impatience with an ignorant public but also his conviction that cinema is associated with assault and pain. In a stunning anticipation of his pronouncement later in his career that the job of a director is to "put the audience through it," he chastises but also enlightens us about how cinema works by pointing out that members of the audience "are entirely oblivious to the fact that the emotions from which they are suffering—I say 'suffering' because they are temporarily abnormal—have been created for them by the camera." And he goes on to say that the director, in charge of a commercial as well as artistic factory, must also be capable of "assaults" in order to protect what is inevitably a large and risky capital investment.

With so much at stake on all levels, it makes perfect sense that the knowledgeable, dedicated, and experienced director be allowed to preside freely over the alchemy of turning lights, camera, action—and money—into cinema, and "It is no wonder that he appears autocratic. He *is* the autocrat of the studio, and he has *got* to be." The autocrat, however, is anything but one-dimensional, and Hitchcock carefully explains that while "brusqueness" is often necessary and forgivable, he "is not a bully at heart," though he might often seem to be, and is capable of a wide range of behavior depending on the circumstances. All this is visible in his description of the ways he treats actors, envisioned not necessarily as a director's enemy but certainly as part of the raw material that demands "pretty rough handling at times" and must one way or another be kept "under the omnipotent autocrat of the studio." Virginia Valli needed "delicate handling," while Nita Naldi, "the complete vamp" on and off-screen, "was temperamentally fitted to withstand any onslaught" in the battle of filmmaking and didn't require him to mind his "'p's and q's.'" Ivor Novello and Isabel Jeans were "delightfully easy to work" with, but though he "never had to lose his temper to get them into the right pose and really tell a story in action and expression," he gives examples of how he had to "resort to tricks and catch them unawares to get the result I aimed at."

As with his actors, the effective autocrat is imaginative and resourceful but also unhesitatingly imperious when necessary in his treatment of the other large group of people who aspire to be exert their control over cinema: authors, who in Hitchcock's opinion, are inevitably but insistently "all wrong in their ideas when their stories are being filmed." A rose in a field of wheat is a weed, and novelists or playwrights, no matter how justly famous and respected, are useless in a studio if they "fail to appreciate the fact that without a knowledge of their chosen medium they cannot hope to turn out an acceptable story." He briefly acknowledges the value and invites "the co-operation of all who know anything about film stories and their making," but for the most part paints a picture of a horde of unskilled and clueless scenario writers who "bombard" him with scripts that are a nuisance and add up to "a mountain of wasted labour." This is an early draft of what would develop into a characteristic complaint (and prejudice) of Hitchcock's: an unfortunate by-product of his particular definition of "pure cinema" and conception of himself as a multi-faceted and omnipotent director is his constant downplaying of the contributions of writers and other collaborators to his films.

While he puts writers in what he feels is their proper subordinate place, he does not, however, minimize the importance of stories, several of which, he says, he plans to write himself, bypassing the need for writers. He has in mind "two good stories" involving "railways" and "our mercantile marine," and his rather surprising comment that he is specifically attracted to these subjects because they offer "a wealth of possibilities in romance" alerts us to two important points: that romance is at the heart of cinema for Hitchcock, and that he defines this term in his own particular way.[6] In the paragraphs that follow he mentions love and exoticism, two conventional elements of romance, and focuses specifically on defining and stressing the importance of what he identifies as an archetypal romantic subject, the "incentive theme." He admires "the life of incentive, of big endeavour and handsome reward" for young lovers who venture away from home, a subject that "runs through American film" and which he vows to bring to English film.[7] But for all that Hitchcock recognizes that cinema is substantially involved with wish-fulfillment and role-modeling, exotic experiences and an imaginary escape from the mundane, he is reaching to articulate a notion of cinematic "romance" that goes beyond "the banal and highly sentimental" portrayal of the incentive theme, and, not surprisingly, his eye is primarily on how such a story can help film create its uniquely powerful effects, taking audiences "out of themselves" and prompting them to "hug themselves and each other in ecstatic joy under cover of the darkened cinema." We are perhaps used to thinking of Hitchcock as a formalist, primarily concerned with technique and treatment, but here he recognizes that stories "throbbing with life" and "rich in romance" are a vital part of what he envisions and clearly describes, long before Susan Sontag coined the term, as an erotics of cinema, in which the most important drama and romance are to be found not in the making of the film or even in the film itself but in the audience's deep and complex response to the film.

The essay concludes "with a word about my routine," actually a substantial section of ten paragraphs, carefully set up to domesticate the autocrat. Here Hitchcock focuses on activities that require flexibility and patience rather than "bullying" or "coaxing," and the overall impression he leaves us with is that he is a thoroughly dedicated and remarkably genial workaholic. Following up on the statement in "Films We Could Make" that "Film directors live with their pictures" (167), he shows in detail how his home is an extension of rather than an escape from the studio, a place where serious work continues, despite the onslaught of fan letters that "pour in upon my inoffensive head even before I can sit down to breakfast" and constitute an "invasion of what little privacy I get over my eggs and bacon"—an honest complaint as well as perhaps a witty literary homage, confirming that his essay is at least fleetingly indebted to the persona, setting, and title of the well-known collection of essays by Oliver Wendell Holmes, *The Autocrat of the Breakfast-Table* (1858). His complete commitment to the art of filmmaking means that he never has a moment of peace and always keeps his "nose to the grindstone," with no holidays or even Sunday breaks. But, again picking up a familial metaphor also used in "Films We Could Make" (167), he has no regrets. His final words, the culmination of an extraordinarily skillful rhetorical performance, plead for, and I think gain, our respect, admiration, and sympathy: "I am not grumbling. The film is my baby, and who can tire of his baby?"

At one point earlier on he off-handedly remarks that he has no interest in politics, in his films or elsewhere—"they are the last things I would discuss anywhere"—but "An Autocrat of the Studio" is from beginning to end about what we can call, without stretching the term too far, the politics of filmmaking. The essay is practical and aesthetic, focusing on how films are and should be made, but also ideological, analyzing the vectors of power in the cinematic apparatus and rationalizing and defending his own claim to be the legitimate and undisputed authority, in part by very shrewd self-representation. We should go directly to Hitchcock's films to see the extent to which he is a master of the art of cinema, but closely examining essays like this one gives us extremely valuable insight into how he is a master of the even broader realm of *res cinematica*.

Notes

1. Donald Spoto, *The Dark Side of Genius: The Life of Alfred Hitchcock* (New York: Ballantine Books, 1983), 120. Further quotations from this book are indicated by page number in parentheses in the body of the text.
2. Patrick McGilligan, *Alfred Hitchcock: A Life in Darkness and Light* (New York: ReganBooks, 2003), 99. Further quotations from this book are indicated by page number in parentheses in the body of the text.
3. Alfred Hitchcock, "Films We Could Make" (1927), in *Hitchcock on Hitchcock: Selected Writings and Interviews*, ed. Sidney Gottlieb (Berkeley and Los Angeles: University of California Press, 1995), 167. For other comments by Hitchcock on the idea that films should be under the control of one person, see "If I Were Head of a Production Company (1935), 173, "Directors Are Dead" (1937), 184, and "Director's Problems" (1938), 187, all in *Hitchcock on Hitchcock*.
4. McGilligan notes that the salary figure announced by B.I.P.—which he specifies as "seventeen thousand pounds annually, for twelve pictures over the next three years"—"was an exaggeration," but one with an immediate salutary effect: "The public vote of confidence gave Hitchcock a brief, rose-colored opportunity to sketch his ambitions for the future" (*Alfred Hitchcock: A Life in Darkness and Light*, 101). McGilligan does not cite "An Autocrat of the Film Studio," but his words describe it and a key part of its origin perfectly.
5. Spoto notes that Hitchcock "only rarely referred to his mother—outside his films—and when he did so in conversation, it

was only in the briefest and most general way" (*The Dark Side of Genius*, 16). Given that, Hitchcock's specific comments on her in this essay are particularly valuable and revealing, and nicely supplement the few stories he usually told about her, especially the most often repeated one about his nightly ritual at "the foot of his mother's bed" where he made an "evening confession" about the "business of the day" (16-17). A full picture of their complex relationship needs to take into account how Hitchcock both relied on her support—Spoto describes him at one point as "a clever, lonely boy, pampered by a doting mother" (22)—and bridled at what he may have perceived as her imperiousness and foolishness.

6. Three essential critical works explore in great detail the different ways that "romance" and "the romantic" figure in Hitchcock's works: Robin Wood, *Hitchcock's Films Revisited*, rev. ed. (New York: Columbia University Press, 2002); Lesley Brill, *The Hitchcock Romance: Love and Irony in Hitchcock's Films* (Princeton: Princeton University Press, 1988); and most recently, Richard Allen, *Hitchcock's Romantic Irony* (New York: Columbia University Press, 2007).

7. In these paragraphs, Hitchcock expands on his brief comments in "Films We Could Make" about the differences between English and American films, currently much to the advantage of the Americans, and the need for English directors to "tell stories of *English* boys who leave the village and make good in the big city" (165) as well as other national dramas, including ones about "the mercantile marine" (166). Hitchcock was never shy about repeating himself in print, and it is worth examining closely how "An Autocrat of the Studio" elaborates on many of the key points introduced in "Films We Could Make."

ALFRED HITCHCOCK

An Autocrat of the Film Studio

The most important development of the film will be its entire severance from both the stage and the novel, and the command of a medium of its own. It should be a medium of itself, and cannot reach what I should call absolute perfection until it can function irrespective of the book and the stage. That is to say, it must be capable of telling a story in its own way, which will be in a way different from both the stage and the novel. To-day it takes something from both.

A New Development

How is this change to be brought about? As near as I can describe it I should say by the substitution of a series of moving tableaux which tell a story without the aid of titles and captions. Experiments in this direction have not so far been remarkable for their success, but that does not disprove the desirability of the development. And for my part I shall do what I can to develop the film along these lines. It is a practical proposition and an achievement worth striving after.

So far as I can see at present the only other developments possible are on the mechanical side. The ideal film will be the coloured stereoscopic film. This perfect film may come in fifty or thirty years. I do not hold out much hope of it coming sooner.

Reprinted from *Cassell's Magazine*, January 1928, 28-34, with the spelling in the original retained and several small errors silently corrected. The six illustrations with captions and the brief headnote are not included. I am grateful to Nancy F. and James M. Vest for providing me with a copy of this article.

But when it has arrived, and we have also the film which tells its own story without the aid of titles or captions, we shall have an entertainment with an identity all its own and capable of commanding equal attention with the theatre and the novel.

So much for the film. Now for a word two about personalities. First and foremost I should like it to be more widely known that a film director does not select casts for his pictures. At least, not in the way a vast congregation of film aspirants seem to think. They bombard me mercilessly with letters setting out their remarkable qualifications for making a name on the films.

An ideal film face is not necessarily superbly beautiful without artificial aids. It must be a strong face. That is, one with the features so clearly cut that the lights and shadows of photography get a real chance. The mouth, chin and forehead must be well formed and the eyes fairly deeply set. Each feature must be definite and firm, yet there must be a mobility of expression covering the whole range of human feelings or emotions, from mild surprise to a tornado of rage, from lukewarm interest to devouring passion.

Next to the face the legs are the most important part of the anatomy. The film aspirant of the fair sex must have a shapely pair of legs, or legs which match the character to be played. This is not to satisfy a special interest of any section of the community, as might—I am not going to be dogmatic about it—as might be the case with revue choruses. Don't forget the camera in film work. In this matter of personal appearance it is more a question of correct focus and lights and shades than a pleasing general appearance.

This would be plain to all if only cinema audiences would pay films the compliment of a more critical observation. If only the public would give the photoplay the same serious attention they give to stage plays, they would see these things for themselves. Unfortunately they will not—not yet, at all events. They are so careless and unobservant that it is only a case of "going to the pictures." Many do not even trouble to discover the titles of the films before taking their seats.

Early Memories

My own mother has been to cinema shows in this casual way and vaguely felt a grudge against somebody or other because she found she had already seen the films. This is a flippant indifference which makes me very angry at times, more especially because it seems as if the public, my own mother among them, cannot take the film seriously. It is a grave fault and an injustice to a work of art and an industry worthy of intelligent support.

Perhaps I feel so keenly about it because films have always been important to me. Even as a boy I never went to a cinema merely for the sake of exciting entertainment. I studied films while taking my pleasure out of them. I formed the habit of thinking in the terms of the film wherever I went. I never saw a play in a theatre without automatically visualising the play as a film. With the arrogant bombast of youth—that is, inexperienced youth—I could settle the point immediately as to whether the play would make a good film or not. Similarly I decided which film had and which had not been worth the trouble and expense of creating.

I remember seeing Mrs. Belloc Lowndes's "Who is He?" at the Haymarket and making up my mind there and then that there was a good film in it. That was my view years ago, and although experience taught me to modify that view, I was right in the main. Experience taught me that the stage presentation of the story would need to be drastically altered for the film, but the idea remained perfectly sound as a film proposition. Around this idea I evolved "The Lodger," familiar by now to millions of cinema-goers. As a boy I saw possibilities in the play for the screen. As a man in my twenties I directed it— which was something the boy certainly did not dream of.

I tell this story only to illustrate my point, that when you take the trouble to study the film—a mental exercise which will not diminish your enjoyment by a fraction, but rather tend to increase it—you will really learn something about it. You will see in it more than you dream of at present.

The astonishing thing to me is that with all their indifference to the points which make or mar a film the public remain susceptible to their influence. By some miracle of sub-conscious understanding they know when a film is good and when another is bad. It is the director's business to know how to produce the film which embodies all those points likely to meet with the approval of his critical yet untaught public. He is a kind of film father providing for his family. The family know what they like, but are sublimely ignorant of all that has gone to the making of their feast.

Let me disillusion them about one detail. All the romance is in the story, not in the film making. The average applicant for a film test has no idea at all of the workaday, unromantic atmosphere of a studio. It is nothing more than an "emotion factory." Emotions of many varying sorts, shades, degrees and colours have to be *manufactured*, and all must be photographically clear. There are innocent people abroad who sincerely believe they can portray a vast range of emotions with little or no experience before the camera. They see only the finished product, the completely *manufactured article* on the screen; they are swayed by the emotions photographed for their benefit and on the way home earnestly tell themselves and each other "they are sure they could act for the film."

They are entirely oblivious to the fact that the emotions from which they are suffering—I say "suffering" because they are temporarily abnormal—have been created for them by the camera, that before they came under the influence of the combined attack of the director, the artistes and the camera, their emotional nature lay dormant. If they really think they can become so emotional at will and draw sympathetic response from people who have paid away good money to see the show, let them give a dumb play before their friends. When they can do this in the presence of a multitude of distractions, say in the midst of a cabinet making factory with determinedly indifferent people moving about them, and can make their friends love as they love, hate as they hate, laugh as they laugh, cry as they cry, feel with them their every mood and fancy, then will they be justified in saying to themselves, "I am sure I can act for the film." All I say is, let them try. Until they have tried they cannot realise how difficult is this business of "emotion manufacture."

Not only is tremendous patience required to achieve perfection but in the studio the novice must be prepared for the assaults of a very commercially-minded critic in the person of the director. Remember, the director is a business man as well as an artist. He must produce something he can sell; something he has got to sell. And he is not making something which costs only a few thousand pounds, as is the theatrical producer. He has to spend anything from £100,000 to £1,000,000 on one production and he has got to get that money back with a legitimate percentage of profit.

It is no wonder that he appears autocratic. He *is* the autocrat of the studio, and he has *got* to be. His brusqueness, which may make it hard for the lovers before the camera to act as if they really "meant it," is a natural consequence of his determination to have the thing done properly in view of the enormous loss which follows if it is not done properly. He is not a bully at heart, but the novice might be forgiven for thinking he is. The star, always a person with experience, knows differently, but the star is no less than the novice subject to some pretty rough handling at times. All come under the omnipotent autocrat of the studio.

Not that cave-man methods are the only sort employed. It depends upon the temperament of the artiste, whether he is brusque or persuasive. It certainly does not depend upon the status of the artiste. Once the director has made up his mind how to get the best from the artiste—whether world-famous star or unknown novice—he adapts his methods to the nature of temperament of the individual. With some the gentle, persuasive method is best. With others only a raging, tearing temper will bring them into his line. The director must therefore be a student of psychology as well as an artist and a business man.

Virginia Valli was a type to be cajoled. Not because she was a great star, but because her temperament was such that rough treatment upset her and she could not give of her best. On the screen she was a lively vivacious character and played the part splendidly. Actually her's was a quiet, subdued nature which called for delicate handling.

Nita Naldi, whom I have always regarded as the world's greatest "vampire," was entirely opposite to Virginia Valli. Off the screen site she was as vivacious as Miss Valli was subdued. On the screen she was a cold, calculating, measuring vamp. Indeed, she was what we call the complete vamp. That is, she could play all kinds of "vampire" parts brilliantly—the baby vamp, meaning a girl in her teens; the youthful vamp; one a few years older and less obvious in her methods; and the vamp which Americans call "the gold digger," the sophisticated woman who can disguise her vamping or indulge in an orgy of it according to the character of the victim.

I never had to mind my "p's" and "q's" with Nita Naldi. Brusqueness did not matter a pin to her. She was temperamentally fitted to withstand any onslaught. She was, too, a wonderful artiste, and now that she has gone to live in retirement in France the cinema world has lost one of its real jewels.

My impression is that the age of the "vampire" has passed. It was a vogue which belonged to the early days of the film and nowadays people do not care for obvious vamping. They do not object to being made fully aware of the intentions of the love-thief, but sheer, blatant vamping is no longer interesting. The subtle, cajoling woman who is fighting for her love with no mercenary motive at all is preferred to the obvious vamp. She has in a sense replaced the vamp.

Whether it is a reflection of the times I am not prepared to say, but if the popularity of film stories implies anything at all, it is that love counts more to-day with women than sheer pelf. Women will sympathise with a woman struggling to get possession of the man she loves, even though she has no moral right to him. On the other hand, they have little patience with the type who merely want the men who can give them an abundance of this world's goods.

Making Her Smile!

Ivor Novello and Isabel Jeans are two other artistes with whom I have found it delightfully easy to work. It has been unnecessary for me to watch for foibles which must be avoided to get the best from these two artistes. Sometimes I have had to resort to tricks and catch them unawares to get the result I aimed at, but I have never had to lose my temper to get them into the right pose and really tell a story in action and expression.

The most I have had to do with Isabel Jeans has been to recite a childhood legend to make her smile in her sleep. That happened when I had her tucked up in bed in a scene in "Easy Virtue." She had to smile through her dreams. She smiled several times, but it was not the sort of smile I wanted. I cannot explain in cold print the infinite varieties of the smile, but this time I wanted one belonging rightfully to innocent slumber and peaceful dreaming.

To repeat the legend would spoil the story and might interfere with the effect when you see the film—that is, for those of you who have not already seen it. Besides, one cannot reproduce here the atmosphere of the setting when the scene was "shot." I tell the story only to illustrate my remark that a simple device of this sort was all I needed to aid me in getting from Miss Jeans just the exact expression I wanted.

The Awkward Author

I might tell some stories of dealings with authors who have to be convinced that they are all wrong in their ideas when their stories are being filmed. As a rule they are all wrong, but it would be better to be tactfully silent as to individuals. I would certainly never employ a famous writer to turn out a film story for me. For this reason, famous writers are artistes who write by inspiration. When they write to order they are so far below their best that it is ten chances to one they will turn out poorer stuff than the gifted hack. But then I do not favour writing to order by anyone. If there is a story in a man's brain he will tell it, and it is almost bound to be worth the telling. And if he is writing for the film with a knowledge of his medium it will be well worth filming.

Scenario writers, or rather a multitude of people who send me scenarios, fail to appreciate the fact that without a knowledge of their chosen medium they cannot hope to turn out an acceptable story. All you good and kind literary people who bombard me with scenarios can place me everlastingly in your debt by holding on to your scripts until you have mastered more technical details. And, incidentally, you will save yourself a mountain of wasted labour.

Naturally, I want the co-operation of all who know anything about film stories and their making, but those who know nothing are worse than a hindrance to themselves and to me. Now I will tell you a secret. I want two good stories. But I am sorry to disappoint you. I am going to write them myself.

One will be about railways and the other about our mercantile marine. Both are magnificent services with a wealth of possibilities in romance. Neither has been exploited in English films. For obvious reasons I cannot say more at present. Perhaps I have said too much as it is.

So far as the English film is concerned, I am convinced that it lacks the incentive theme and, therefore, lags behind the American. Artistically, the English film is as good as anything turned out in America. But in how many American films do you see the village youth leaving home, fighting adversity, winning his way through and finally returning to live near his native cottage, but in marble halls and with the girl of his youth adorning the magnificence in beautiful bridal array!

It may be all banal and highly sentimental, exaggerated even to flunkeys, but there is something incentive about it all. The young man and the young woman, ardent lovers, see themselves in the places of the hero and heroine and they enjoy a wonderful journey through the flowering, perfumed land of make-believe. They hug themselves and each other in ecstatic joy under cover of the darkened cinema, and then − − − ?

What happens? They resume their ordinary daily English round, coming to earth with a bump and realise that in their lives there is no real incentive. Politics apart−and they are the last thing I would discuss anywhere−where is the incentive in British industry? Perhaps characteristic English home-life is the wrong kind of soil for the incentive plant to flourish in, being too home-spun.

The life of incentive, of big endeavour and handsome reward, runs through the American film, and because it is something different from the run of things in England,

English youths flock to see the American film. It takes them out of themselves and gives them something to look at which is utterly different from what they can themselves experience. There is a marvellous field of opportunities for the English producer who will try to understand the characteristics of his own people and work from the clues they give him. Million and two-million pound spectacular productions are not needed. Our people want stories throbbing with life, magnificent in effort, clean in humour and rich in romance. And that I believe I shall continue to put into practice as a director.

Let me close with a word about my own routine. Both at home and at the studio there is always a large post to be gone through. The more persistent among the ambitious ferret out my home address, with the result that letters pour in upon my inoffensive head even before I can sit down to breakfast.

As a hint to those concerned, I may add that the invasion of what little privacy I get over my eggs and bacon does not help their cause.

By nine-thirty every morning I am at the studio, and there I delve once again into a prodigious mail. But the subsequent sorting out of letters I have to leave to my secretary. Those dealing with scenarios go to the story department, and applications for employment on the screen go to the casting department—if they go anywhere at all.

Dealing with Temperament

Then I go to the projection theatre where I inspect all the sets photographed the previous day. I think it is common knowledge that each set has to be photographed several times, which, incidentally, adds a respectable lump to the total mountain of expense in making a film. The several sets are run off before me and I then select the best. If none come up to scratch, the set has to be acted over again several more times.

This is not necessarily caused by inefficiency of the artistes. Sometimes they are not in the mood for the particular work in hand. As a rule I can detect temperamental defects during a setting, and when I do, the filming is abandoned.

Neither "bullying" nor coaxing will avail in such circumstances. If the artistes are, as it were, out of gear, it is better to send them home. I do.

The previous day's work reviewed, I pass them to the "floor," or the stage where the acting is done, and inspect the make-up of artistes detailed for the day's filming. My production secretary will have already decided upon the section of the story to be photographed and ordered the attendance of artistes.

A Day's Work

Stars do not attend this inspection, for they can generally be trusted to make-up properly. Sometimes they fail, and when they do they also have to retire and re-makeup. It is essential that all taking part in the day's work before the camera must be perfectly made-up, otherwise the lights and shades would be out of joint.

Next I go through the day's work mapped out by my production secretary—sometimes called "floor" secretary. She keeps a complete diary of the details of the production, of the artistes who have to be called and the possible order of filming the story.

These tasks usually fill in the morning and there is an hour's break for lunch. At two o'clock I deal with interviewers, and it would surprise some people how many interviews I can get through in the allotted half-hour. The afternoon is given up to "shooting" scenes or sets until six or seven p.m., after which I spend an hour going over "takes" and selecting the best for connected exhibition the next morning. Nine o'clock, dinner at home and then "house" interviews. That is, if anybody has been lucky enough to force me to break a rule.

I object to working more than twelve hours a day, but sometimes it can't be avoided. Holidays! I never take them like other people. Since January 1st I have had three days off. All the others, including Sundays, I have been compelled to keep my nose to the grindstone. But I am not grumbling. The film is my baby, and who can tire of his baby?

MICHAEL WALKER

A Perfect Place to Die?
The Theater in Hitchcock Revisited

If one looks up the various entries listed under "Theater" in the bibliography index of Jane Sloan's admirable reference work, *Alfred Hitchcock: The Definitive Filmography*, one discovers that almost all of them are about "the theatrical" in Hitchcock; in other words, they look *thematically* at notions of "theater" in his films.[1] The significance of the use of the theater as a *setting* in his movies has been less explored. I am aware of only one major article on this subject, "A Perfect Place to Die: Theater in Hitchcock's Films" by Alenka Zupančič.[2] The main thread of Zupančič's argument is encapsulated in her title; that, in a number of Hitchcock films, the climax occurs in a theater and includes an onstage death: "the stage is a place of truth and a place of death" (79). Taking this observation as my starting point, I would like to look in more detail at Hitchcock's theater scenes. I will begin by running through Zupančič's examples, which are not in fact confined to actual theaters, but include a range of "theater-type" settings.

The Theater Death Scene

Zupančič cites four films in which a "theater death scene" is the climax. In *Murder!* (1930), Fane (Esme Percy) commits suicide during a trapeze performance in the circus ring. In *The 39 Steps* (1935), Mr. Memory (Wylie Watson) is shot during an onstage performance at the London Palladium. In *Stage Fright* (1950), Jonathan (Richard Todd) is killed by a falling safety curtain on stage. In *I Confess* (1953), Keller (O.E. Hasse) is cornered by the police in an empty hotel ballroom, and although Zupančič is wrong in stating that he's shot and dies on the stage (73), he does shoot from the stage and he's shot while standing next to it. Of these four examples, Zupančič notes that, in each case, the scene includes (a) the suspect confronted with "representatives of the law," (b) an admission of guilt and (c) "the execution of the sentence" (81).

There are in fact other climactic "theater" scenes which Zupančič mentions in passing (73) and which could be included here. In both versions of *The Man Who Knew Too Much* (1934, 1955) there is an attempted assassination during a concert in the Albert Hall in London. In both cases, the attempt is only narrowly averted, and results in a wounding. In addition, the assassin in the remake is himself seemingly killed, falling from a box into the stalls. The climax of *Young and Innocent* (1937) occurs in a dance hall, and begins with a famous crane and dolly shot which moves over the dance floor to end on the twitching eye of the film's murderer, Guy (George Curzon), who is the drummer in a band on stage. Although the scene does not culminate with a death, it fits in with the others: it ends with the murderer's confession and arrest, and he will presumably go on to legal execution.

The one major climactic theater scene which Zupančič ignores is that in *Torn Curtain* (1966). In this case, the events do not fit her schema: although a performance is dramatically interrupted, no one is killed (or apprehended). This exception opens up a gap in her argument that I'd like to explore. First I will look at her examples and consider what would seem to lie behind this striking connection in Hitchcock between the theater and death scenes. And second I will look at those theater scenes that do not conform to her thesis, and consider why.

On the first point, it can be seen that these scenes occur above all in the falsely-accused man films. These "wrong man" films constitute one of Hitchcock's most familiar plots: the police are convinced that the hero (in one case, *Murder!*, the heroine) is guilty of murder, and pursue him/her rather than the real murderer. The false attribution of guilt persists throughout the film, and is indeed made public: e.g., an actual conviction for murder in *Murder!*, newspaper and radio reports in *The 39 Steps*. Accordingly, it would seem that Hitchcock also seeks to make the identification of the true villain public, and the theater is an excellent setting in which to effect this. It is in full view of an audience that the real murderer is revealed, and even if the audience does not understand what is going on, it is there to bear witness to the moment of revelation. This idea could be seen to lie behind Fane's suicide in *Murder!*, the onstage exposé of Mr. Memory and master spy Jordan (Godfrey Tearle) in *The 39 Steps*, and the identification of the murderer in *Young and Innocent*. And, in the first two films, exposure of the villain(s) also involves a violent death.

In fact, *Murder!* has a double operation in this regard. After the villain's death in the circus ring—and the subsequent reading of his confession by Sir John (Herbert Marshall)—we then see the heroine Diana (Norah Baring) on stage, acting with Sir John in a play that tells "the true story" of the case in which she was involved. Just as the circus audience was present to bear witness to the revelation of the real murderer, so the theater audience bears witness to the innocence of the falsely-accused heroine. The presence here of two "theater" scenes emphasizes that the "theater death scene" is in fact part of a wider Hitchcock paradigm, one which uses the theater not simply as "a place of death" but also as a place of public revelation.

The climax in the London Palladium in *The 39 Steps* is the classic example in Hitchcock where the whole "theater climax paradigm" (as I'll call it) is played out in one theater setting. The basic ingredients of the scene are also typical of the climax in a Hitchcock thriller: the falsely-accused hero, Hannay (Robert Donat), is in pursuit of the real villains (here spies); the police are in pursuit of the hero. Accordingly, all the main characters are present in the theater: Hannay and Pamela (Madeleine Carroll) are in the stalls; Jordan is in a box close to the stage; Mr. Memory is on stage; the police are everywhere. But it is Hannay who is privileged with "the power of the look": through opera glasses, he first spots Jordan, then a signal between Jordan and Memory. This enables him to work out the spies' plan. However, as policemen move in to arrest him, they refuse to listen to him. Hannay can only redirect them towards the real villains by shouting out a question to Memory: "What are the 39 steps?" Obliged to answer, Memory starts to talk about the spy network, whereupon Jordan shoots him. His box exit blocked by a policeman, he then leaps onto the stage. Police promptly close in on him from all sides. The wounded Memory is led off to the wings, where, as chorus girls dance in the background, Hannay prompts him to reveal, in front of the police, that he's memorized state secrets. The garbled recitation functions as his confession. He then, seemingly, dies. Standing in respectful silence beside his body, Hannay and Pamela hold hands.

All the elements of the film are brought to a resolution in this *dénouement*, and the theater is an ideal arena to do this: to expose the villains, enlighten the hitherto misguided police, clear the hero's name, and give the hero and heroine a happy ending. In this respect, the theater may be seen as a setting in which a number of different narrative elements may readily be gathered together, and I will mention later connections between this theater scene and the one at the beginning of the film. Here I wish to note the points relevant to the paradigm. First, the scene includes Zupančič's three basic ingredients: the presence of the police, the admission of guilt, and "the execution of the sentence." Second, it also includes the witnessing audience, who are not panicked into fleeing from the theater, like their Music Hall predecessors in the opening theater scene, but are calmed by the dancing girls. Third, picking up on a point from my article in *Hitchcock Annual* 15 on the power of the superego figures in Hitchcock, we could note that the stage is also the place where the superego figures "swoop": Jordan shoots Mr. Memory; the police close in on Jordan.[3]

This introduces another feature of the paradigm: the figure on the stage is also typically subject to a severe, judgmental pressure which is like the edict of the superego. The police presence is usually only a part of this, and in *Murder!*, for example, the police are not even there, so that Sir John alone is the superego figure. Fane knows that Sir John knows that he is a murderer, and so as Sir John watches him intently from the audience below, Fane experiences Sir John's gaze as accusatory. In *The 39 Steps*, Jordan functions as Mr. Memory's criminal superego, punishing him for talking. The police are more conventional superego figures, but their emergence to seize Jordan is so swift that it's almost comical. It's as though the stage is being policed by a superego force, just waiting to pounce on transgression.

Stage Fright offers a variation on the basic structure of these scenes, a variation which supports the point about the significance of the witnessing audience.[4] Here the villain's death is played to an empty theater. But this is entirely appropriate: although we have been led to believe throughout the film that Jonathan was a "wrong man," we have just discovered—he has confessed to the heroine, Eve (Jane Wyman)—that he is, in fact, guilty. The only witnesses to his death are Eve, some theater hands, and the police, and all of them are either onstage or in the wings; the actual auditorium is empty. There is no need for a public audience because in this case no shift in popular perceptions is required: the "wrong man" *is* the villain.

Again, however, one might note Freudian overtones to the sequence. The scene between Eve and Jonathan takes place in a theatrical coach *under* the stage: this is the sort of location in Hitchcock which, like the cellar in *Psycho* (1960), topographically implies the id. Registering that this is a darker, more threatening scene, Hitchcock films it with *noir* low-key lighting, as Jonathan first confesses to and then threatens murder. Eve then tricks him into going up onto the stage, and the safety curtain which there descends on him is exactly like a superego force, swooping down like a guillotine to execute the guilty figure.

Set in Quebec, *I Confess* offers a more complicated variation of the paradigm. Here the falsely-accused hero is a

Roman Catholic priest, Father Logan (Montgomery Clift), who is tried for the murder of Vilette (Ovila Légaré), a blackmailer. His predicament is bound up with his vocation: the real murderer, Keller, had confessed to him, but he cannot divulge what he heard in confession. Moreover, Logan interprets this edict in wider terms: he refuses to say anything that might lead people to realize that Keller had indeed confessed to him, which might in turn enable them to work out his predicament. (I set aside the fact that the police should have realized this anyway. Inspector Larrue [Karl Malden] is one of Hitchcock's more sensible policeman, but all policemen in Hitchcock fail in some respects.)

Nevertheless, the jury, albeit reluctantly, finds Logan innocent of the murder. However, the judge disagrees, and says so. The disapproval spreads quickly. As Logan is released, Ruth (Anne Baxter) steps towards him, essentially out of sympathy. The courtroom audience hisses. There is clearly a sense of theater to this, supporting the oft-made comparison between the courtroom and the theater.[5] But the audience is not restricted to the courtroom: as Logan walks out of the courthouse, people line the corridors and even confront him in the street outside. And it is in front of these crowds that Keller betrays himself—by shooting and killing his wife Alma (Dolly Haas). Only then does he flee into the hotel, the Château Frontenac, and, finally, the empty ballroom. The ingredients—the witnessing audience and the death in the "theater"—are both there, but split.

The variation strengthens the sense that, when the hero has been falsely-accused, Hitchcock is keen that there is an audience present to bear witness to the identification of the true villain. It is the very people who have been crowding round and even manhandling Logan who discover that the real killer is in their midst, firing a gun. Equally, again there is a significant "mobilization" of superego figures and here the hero, too, is subjected to their judgment. In particular, the moral disapproval of the judge, one such superego figure, spreads to the crowd, so that they are united by a hostility to Logan which makes them seem like a collective malevolent superego, bearing down on him. An analogy may be drawn with the birds in *The Birds* [1963], which Margaret M. Horwitz has likened to a "malevolent female superego."[6] That would suggest why the ending of *I Confess*, which I have discussed elsewhere, gives such prominence to benevolent superego figures.[7] The penultimate shot of the film—before the closing shot of the Château Frontenac—is quite extraordinary: as Logan in close-up prays and then closes the dead Keller's eyes, the low angle of the shot and its shallow focus show the heads of Inspector Larrue and Father Millais (Charles Andre), superego figures both, out of focus above and behind him, as if they were semi-ethereal figures looking down on him.

Variations and Rhetorical Devices

A curious point about Hitchcock's theater scenes is that none is set in the U.S. Obviously this is true of his English period, but it's also true of his Hollywood period. As noted, the Château Frontenac is in Quebec. In *Stage Fright* and *The Man Who Knew Too Much*, the theater or concert hall scenes are in London. The theater scene in *Torn Curtain* is set in East Berlin. In the Hollywood movies, there are occasional American-set theater-type scenes—I'd include a couple of scenes in *North by Northwest* (1959) in this category—but no scene set in an actual theater.

However, there is one film, *Saboteur* (1942), that includes alternatives, specifically a ballroom scene and a cinema scene, and both contain elements relevant to this discussion. The former occurs in the luxury mansion of a New York matriarch, Mrs. Sutton (Alma Kruger), which the hero and heroine discover is actually a hideout for the saboteurs. During a break in the dancing, the falsely-accused hero, Barry (Robert Cummings), goes up to the stage (temporarily vacated by the musicians) and starts to make a speech saying that the house is full of fifth columnists. He is silenced by the threat of being shot, and, as in *The Man Who Knew Too Much*, the gun is discreetly hidden behind a curtain on the balcony. So in this theater-type scene, the threat of death is quite explicit, and the threat is expressed in a self-consciously theatrical way: the gun hidden behind a curtain. Later, the police pursue Fry (Norman Lloyd), the true villain, into a cinema. He ends up on the stage, where he creates much the same sort of public disturbance as in the theater scenes elsewhere in Hitchcock. He and the police even exchange shots in the crowded auditorium, panicking the audience. But, because the film is being shown in the dark, the villain is not being *identified* to the audience in the same way as in the equivalent theater scenes. Hitchcock of course recognized this. The final exposé of the villain occurs later, when he dangles from the hero's hand at the top of the Statue of Liberty and then plunges to his death. Because this occurs in the presence of onlookers, both in the crown of the statue and on the ground, we could describe it as a theater-type scene.

An example which reinforces this sense that the exposé of the true villain should preferably have an audience is the climax of *To Catch a Thief* (1954). In this film, Robie (Cary Grant) is a falsely-accused jewel thief. He finally corners the real thief—who happens to be a woman, Danielle (Brigitte Auber)—on a rooftop. But, markedly more than in *Saboteur*, Hitchcock stages the public revelation of Danielle as the villain as a piece of theater. Again, the hero is holding the villain suspended over a drop to the ground, and here he is forcing her to confess. But in this case, not only are there spectators, including the police, below, but the police are also shining a spotlight on the two of them. Moreover, Robie actually says to Danielle: "You've got a full house down there—begin the performance." He then makes her confess loudly enough for everyone to hear.

Like the spotlights on Fane when he hangs himself in the circus ring, the spotlight here is part of the visual rhetoric of the scene. In these climaxes, it is above all the guilt of the villain that Hitchcock is seeking to expose, and the spotlight is part of this: the guilty person is caught in its beam. In effect, the spotlight is like a visualization of the "accusing gaze" of the superego. There is a similar effect with the camera steadily advancing towards the murderer in *Young and Innocent*; the camera here is a sort of spatial equivalent of a spotlight, picking out the guilty person. In both *The 39 Steps* and *Stage Fright*, there is a high angle shot from the top of the theater as the villain is caught, exposed, either on stage (*The 39 Steps*) or in the orchestra pit (*Stage Fright*), another equivalent of the spotlight shot.

Another standard trope in these scenes is the way the police seem to block all the escape routes: in *The 39 Steps*, for instance, they make a point of closing off all the routes out of the theater. In some cases, as in *Young and Innocent*, this may be essentially a subjective impression: the murderer *thinks* that he sees the police closing in on him, and this exacerbates his guilt. He begins to drum more and more erratically, eventually having a mental collapse on the stage and then confessing. In others, as in *Stage Fright*, the police really may be surrounding and advancing on the villain: when Jonathan is caught on stage, point-of-view shots show that all the exits he looks towards have police—or, in one case, a stage hand—blocking the way.

Collectively, these rhetorical devices—the spotlights, the spotlight shots, the (point-of-view) shots of police at the exits—combine to create what may be termed a paranoid structure. This of course occurs elsewhere in Hitchcock, e.g., in *Strangers on a Train* (1951), where there are many shots of Bruno (Robert Walker) from the point of view of Guy (Farley Granger), shots in which the paranoid structure is conveyed through Bruno's direct look at the camera.[8] The significance of the structure here is that it is associated with the theater, specifically with being on stage, and especially when the "representatives of the law" make an appearance, as they tend to do at the climax of the "wrong man" films. A theatrical space is a perfect setting in which to capture this quintessentially Hitchcockian experience: the sense of being trapped (by the law) and caught in a network of (accusing) gazes. This subjective sense of being trapped adds another feature to the theater climax paradigm.[9]

A theater-type scene which introduces an interesting variation on the sense of being trapped is the auction room sequence in *North by Northwest*. The scene is significant in a number of ways: it's the first time that Roger (Cary Grant) sees the villain Vandamm (James Mason) and the heroine Eve (Eva Marie Saint) together; it also includes the introduction of the MacGuffin. But again there is a performance, the auction, which Roger has to disrupt in order to escape, because in this case the spies are blocking all the exits. And so Roger provokes a disturbance in order to *summon* the police. However, he's not a typical falsely-accused man. Although the police think that he's a murderer, also in the auction room audience is the Professor (Leo G. Carroll), who knows that he isn't. Nevertheless, the Professor is the superego figure here, and he views with alarm the way in which Roger is jeopardizing the U.S. Intelligence Agency's plans by drawing attention, not just to himself, but to his romantic relationship with Eve. And so, after the police have arrested—and thereby rescued—Roger, he steps in.

The auction room scene turns into a comic variation of the paradigm. The spies blocking the exits are discombobulated, the middle-class patrons of the event are outraged, and the hero is led off under arrest but still has time to pause and joke with one of the spies: "Sorry, old man. Too bad, keep trying." However, the Professor is not amused. Accordingly, he sets up a second theater-type scene, the cafeteria scene, in which he makes certain that he controls the performance. This ensures that his idea of order is restored. The power of the superego figure in Hitchcock is, once again, clearly shown.

The Albert Hall climax in *The Man Who Knew Too Much* (both versions) is a more oblique example of the paradigm. The dynamics of the scene are different from the other theater climaxes: here the stage is occupied by the orchestra, which is only involved in the violence insofar as the assassin is going to use the clash of the cymbals to conceal the sound of his gunshot. The violence itself is within the auditorium: a shot fired from one box to another across the stalls. Nevertheless, it is still within a theatrical space that the assassination attempt takes place, as though, once again, the structure of the auditorium—the would-be victim exposed in one box; the assassin able to take aim from behind the curtains in another box—lends itself to murder.

It is now possible to consider the significance of the variations to the paradigm in *Torn Curtain*. On stage is a ballet performance of Tchaikovsky's "fantasy" *Francesca di Rimini*, with its lovers in the circles of Hell. In the audience are Michael (Paul Newman) and Sarah (Julie Andrews), waiting for the opportunity to escape backstage. However, although, as in *The 39 Steps*, the hero is with the heroine in the stalls, here he is not a wrong man, he is guilty: guilty of murder, guilty of stealing state secrets.[10] It is only because he has done both these in a Communist country that the film seeks to save him. So the theater scene has a different dynamic: the guilty figure is not on stage but in the audience, and the East German police who appear in the theater are here after the right man.

There are a number of points relevant to these variations. First, Michael is spotted in the audience by a ballerina (Tamara Toumanova) dancing on stage: Hitchcock uses flash freezes as she pirouettes to signal her exceptionally sharp observation. When she goes offstage and points Michael out to the stage manager, it's her eye we see in close-up through a peephole. In other words, here a woman on stage is given "the power of the look," and because of the implications of that power—she supports the Communist regime—it locates her as the accusing superego figure, gazing down on the guilty figure. Second, whereas Sarah watches the ballet intently, Michael can barely look at it. Of course, he may be registering stereotypical male boredom at being obliged to watch a ballet, but perhaps his guilty conscience is disturbed by the image of Hell on stage. Third, when police appear at the exit points, it is the hero who sees them this way: as the guilty figure, here he is made the focus of the paranoid structure. Fourth, when, in order to escape, Michael creates audience panic by pointing at the paper flames of Hell on stage and shouting "Fire!," he is not transforming the theater into "a place of truth," but a place of chaos. Because the interruption is thrown across the footlights, as it were, this is the equivalent of Hannay's question, "What are the 39 steps?," but it is designed to serve the opposite function. All these variations and reversals in the material of the theater climax paradigm serve to stress the crucial moral difference in this scene: the hero is not a falsely-accused innocent; he really is a murderer.

The Stage as Female Space

The variation that I would like to focus on in this section is the fact that the central figure on the stage in *Torn Curtain* is a woman. In all the other examples of the theater climax paradigm, the central figure on the stage is a man. Even in the marginal example of *To Catch a Thief*, Danielle is disguised as a man. This would suggest that, in order to explore the paradigm further, we should look at the other theater scenes in Hitchcock, many of which feature women on the stage, or, as in *Torn Curtain*, center on a woman, with men as secondary performers.

In fact, a number of Hitchcock's heroines actually work on the stage, and so theater scenes recur throughout these films. This goes back to the first scene of his first film, *The Pleasure Garden* (1926), which may indeed be seen as exemplary. As chorus girls dance on stage, an elderly man in the front row uses opera glasses to inspect Patsy (Virginia Valli), the heroine. However, as he ogles her, she challenges his look and shortly afterwards, when he comes backstage to meet her, she has little difficulty in embarrassing him. In short, Hitchcock makes it clear that, while on stage, Patsy remains in control. So, from the beginning of his career, Hitchcock presents the stage as female territory. Although the background power of the Pleasure Garden proprietor Oscar Hamilton (George Snell) should also be recognized here, when it comes to a performance, the women "control" the stage space. In brief, women are at home on the stage; men are not.

The implications of this run through most if not all of the "theater" scenes in Hitchcock. Stage performances which center on women are in general harmonious. They may well be interrupted, as in *Torn Curtain*, but that is almost always because a man with his own agenda is creating a disturbance. By contrast, men on stage bring trouble. Either they introduce a threat of some sort or, more often, they themselves are subjected to a threat, which leads to violence. It is as though there is something wrong with the very idea of a man being on stage, especially if he is performing before an audience.

The contrast between stage scenes centering on women and those featuring men can be clarified by looking at the earlier theater scenes in the films with the theater climax paradigm. *Murder!* begins with a murder within a theater troupe: one actress is killed; another, Diana, is arrested for the crime. During the film, there are then examples of both a theater and a theater-type scene before the climax in the circus. In the former, two policemen are questioning the other members of the troupe about what happened on the night of the murder. But, in a characteristic Hitchcock example of the police conducting their investigations in the most clodhopping way, they do this during a performance. And so their questions are forever being interrupted by the actors going on and coming off the stage.

We stay in the wings during this, and only see fragments of the play (a farce) which is being enacted on the stage in the background. This is an unusual theater scene: it has little of the interaction between audience and performance of the typical scenes. It serves, rather, to introduce a number of the characters in the troupe, one of whom is Fane, who will turn out to be the murderer. Moreover, he walks offstage and into the film dressed as a woman. Although this is primarily a signifier of his ambiguous gender status in the film, it may also be seen as a comment on the sort of man who feels at home on stage.[11] At the same time, the scene may be viewed as showing the resistance of "the theater" to the concerns of the police, as the performance cheerily goes on despite their dogged questioning. What might have been an example of the police dragging the issue of murder into the theater is turned into a comic scene in which the theater troupe goes about its business unperturbed by such matters. In this example, the contaminating effect of men intruding onstage is held at bay.

By contrast, in the theater-type scene, which only involves men, murder is a central concern. Sir John sets up an audition in which he tries to get Fane to act out how the murder itself was carried out. This is done like "The Mousetrap" scene in *Hamlet*, in an attempt to trick the murderer into betraying himself. In effect, this is a theatrical recreation of the lead-up to the murder itself. In a clear example of the negative associations of men and the theater, a theater-type scene exclusively involving men refers explicitly to murder.

The opening theater scene in *The 39 Steps* is similarly revealing. The film begins with Hannay entering a music hall, where one of the acts is Mr. Memory. However, during Mr. Memory's performance, a major disturbance occurs in the auditorium. There is a bar in the stalls, and trouble breaks out with some drunken patrons: a fight ensues which spreads to the audience. Here the men on the stage, including Mr. Memory, call for calm, but the fight continues. Then someone fires a gun, and everyone stampedes out of the theater. Here the theater does indeed become a setting for violence, but my point is that it is when a man is on stage that this occurs.

At the climax in the Palladium, it is again when Mr. Memory is on stage that violence erupts in the theater. However, unlike the music hall audience, the Palladium audience is then calmed down, and what calms it is the chorus girls. Harmony is restored when, once more, the stage becomes female space. There is clearly an ideological operation here. We can see why chorus girls on stage are not a threat: they are a spectacle, entertaining the (implicitly male) audience through their dance routine and skimpy costumes. The same principle would seem to extend to female performers in general: they are being looked at, which supports the dominant ideology. This does not mean that Hitchcock simply reinforces the ideology: the opening sequence of *The Pleasure Garden* actually subverts the female exhibitionist/male voyeur dynamic. Nevertheless, there is a sense that women on stage are pleasing, not disturbing. But why should the stage setting seem so dangerous for men? Before it is possible to suggest an answer to this, it is necessary to look at the other pre-climax theater scenes in Hitchcock. In fact, *The 39 Steps* also includes another of these scenes. At one point, Hannay makes a political speech on a stage platform—and survives. The scene is something of an exception in Hitchcock's work, and it is perhaps significant that it only occurs after Hannay has been shot and left for dead. Clearly he leads a charmed life. Nevertheless, at the end of the scene, Hannay promptly passes into the hands of the spies, who kidnap him. The threat of death is still there; it's just postponed.

The theater scenes in *Stage Fright* strengthen the sense that the stage is female space, and that men in this environment are not merely disruptive, but are also prone to introduce the taint of murder. As in *Murder!*, the film begins with a murder, and the hunt for the killer is the main focus of the narrative. In this case, the victim is the husband of a famous singing star, Charlotte Inwood (Marlene Dietrich). Moreover, the film's heroine, Eve, is a drama student. Accordingly, there are theater scenes throughout the narrative. In the first of these, Eve is interrupted during a drama school rehearsal by her boyfriend, Jonathan, who is in flight from the police. In fact, this interruption leads to nothing more serious than the wrath of the teacher in charge of the rehearsal, who promptly expels the students from the stage—a superego intervention, to be sure, but hardly a deadly one. Nevertheless, Jonathan walks onto the stage with blood on his hands; it is just that we don't yet know this.

In two later theater scenes, Charlotte sings on stage. During the first, Jonathan again threatens to disrupt the performance—he appears in the West End theater as Charlotte is singing—but Charlotte keeps her poise and does not reveal that she has seen him. The second scene goes further. It occurs in a marquee at a garden party; a temporary theater. As Charlotte is singing "La Vie en Rose," a cub scout goes onto the stage and holds up a doll with a bloody dress in front of her. This is an explicit reminder of her husband's murder, and she is unable to continue singing. Here a reference to murder does indeed disrupt the performance. Again, however, the interruption has been staged by a man: Eve's father, who, convinced that Charlotte killed her husband, wants to force her to confess. And so, here he is the superego figure. At the same time, all the interruptions of women on stage in *Stage Fright* are from men who are pursuing their own agendas at the expense of a concern for the woman.

It is also extremely rare for a Hitchcock hero to perform on stage. Although Sir John in *Murder!* is both a playwright and an actor, the final brief scene is the only time we see him act in public. There is, I think, only one developed Hitchcock theater scene in which we see the film's hero in a public performance. This occurs in *Downhill* (1927), a silent movie, and the scene is preceded by an intertitle "The World of Make-Believe." We then see Roddy (Ivor Novello) as a waiter, who, after serving a couple, Julia (Isabel Jeans) and Archie (Ian Hunter), secretly pockets the cigarette case they have left behind. But Hitchcock is teasing us: just as we think that the hero has become a thief, the camera pans across to the couple, who break into a song and dance; it then pans farther to show footlights and a conductor: we now realize that we are witnessing a stage performance. Chorus girls come on from the wings, and the rest of the cast lines up behind them and joins in the dance. Although Julia and Archie downstage continue their number, it is the high-kicking chorus girls behind them whose energy dominates the scene, so that, once again, the stage seems primarily a female space. In particular, Roddy is located at the very back of the stage, accompanying the dance with a rather mechanical bobbing movement. In itself, this is a harmless little scene, but the introductory intertitle nevertheless warns us. This is the beginning of the hero's infatuation with the "false world" of the theater: he goes onto become a victim of the unscrupulousness of Julia and Archie. Once again, when a man is involved, the world of the theater is viewed negatively.

Men who work on the stage in Hitchcock are almost all villains. Archie collaborates with Julia, his girlfriend, in fleecing Roddy of an inheritance. Memory is a traitor; Fane,

Guy in *Young and Innocent*, and Jonathan—who used to be one of Charlotte's back-up dancers—are all murderers. It's as though there is something suspect about a man who earns his living by performing on the stage. As if to stress this, Hitchcock tends to present men on stage in a distinctly unflattering manner. Roddy's bobbing at the back of the crowd in *Downhill* looks silly, especially since he and the man next to him rapidly go out of synchronization with one another. Fane is presented as emasculated: in both the theater and the circus ring, he is shown in drag. Mr. Memory cannot control the audience during his performance in the music hall. Even subsidiary acts involving men tend to look foolish. A slapstick routine preceding Memory's act on the Palladium stage involves men behaving like boisterous children. Apart from the leader, all the members of Guy's band are in blackface, so that they look like caricatures; Guy himself cannot stop his eye twitching. Overall, it's as if there is something unmanly about working on stage, and being subjected to the gaze of the audience. All these male examples contrast with the panache with which Hitchcock's chorus girls dance, or with Charlotte's controlled and stylish singing performances.

Because so many of the villains actually work on the stage, it is also not surprising that the climaxes occur in the theater: Hitchcock contrives that the moment when justice catches up with the villain is during a performance. It is when all eyes are on him—an essential element of the paranoid structure—that the villain is caught. And, for those Hitchcock villains who feel guilt, the sense of being exposed to the law leads to breakdown: Fane commits suicide; Guy has a genuine nervous breakdown.

Politics and Theater

One reason why a number of the scenes involving men on the stage result in violence can be seen in an argument that Ina Rae Hark develops about such scenes in Hitchcock's political films. She writes that "Repeated sequences in the political films portray an audience, in which the amateur sits, and a performance or lecture that the professional enemies of democracy control or manipulate."[12] The sequences she considers are the Albert Hall concert in each version of *The Man Who Knew Too Much* (and the service in the Tabernacle of the Sun in the 1934 version), the Palladium climax in *The 39 Steps*, the Peace Organization banquet in *Foreign Correspondent* (1940), Mrs. Sutton's charity ball in *Saboteur*, the auction in *North by Northwest*, and the ballet in *Torn Curtain*. There is a significant overlap between Hark's examples and mine: only the Tabernacle service and the *Foreign Correspondent* banquet are outside the examples I have been considering.

Hark's basic points offer a useful insight into what is going in some of the theater climaxes. She points out that in the Albert Hall concert and the Palladium, the enemy agents are using the occasion or the setting as a cover for their activities, and in both cases it is a scream or shout from a member of the audience that foils their plot (13). Here the "amateur" in the audience is the heroine or hero, and she/he is the only one who knows what is really going on; the official authorities are more or less wilfully blind. Disrupting the occasion in order to expose "the enemies of democracy" then runs like a thread through Hark's examples. Only the banquet in *Foreign Correspondent* is free from disruption or the threat of it. And so we can see that, in a number of Hitchcock's theater climaxes, violence occurs because the setting has become contaminated by the intrusion of political intrigue into the event. In Hitchcock, political intrigue invariably leads to violence.

Again, however, the *Torn Curtain* climax is different. From the point of view of Cold War politics, Michael's disruption is indeed directed at "the enemies of democracy." But it would be straining things somewhat to argue that he is also the figure who knows what is really going on and that the Communist authorities are blind. As a spy who has killed in order to complete his mission—which is, moreover, personal rather than for his country—it is he who stands accused. Although we want him to escape, he is a deeply compromised hero. As if to underline this, the place where he and Sarah escape to is *under* the stage (a sign in German tells us this). The costume baskets into which they are fastened are thus not only the equivalent of the theatrical coach in *Stage Fright* but also under Dante's Hell on the stage. As for the observant ballerina, her "reward" is the brutal disruption of her ballet.

The Problem of I Confess

Again and again in Hitchcock, there is a sense that the stage is female territory, and that the only sort of men who belong there are either feminized, or villains, or both. This idea can be seen to lie behind almost all the main examples of the "theater climax paradigm." The only film that fits neither this structure nor Hark's is *I Confess*. Here the villain has no connection whatever with the stage. And so, this remains the "problem case," the film which requires separate consideration. This will necessitate a more detailed discussion than the other films.

I would like to start with the opening scene. As the camera cranes in through the window of Vilette's town house, we see his body, splayed on its back in a distinctly sexualized pose, the murder weapon—a metal bar—close by. The camera then pans and tilts up, showing a bead curtain swaying in the doorway: the murderer has just left. This looks like Vilette's study: there is a desk, and a bookcase along the visible wall. There are also four chairs side by side in front of the bookcase; a rather odd detail. But the most unusual feature is the bead curtain. When we return to the house the following day, we can see that the curtain lies, in fact, between the study and an outer room. A number on the outer room door indicates that these were the rooms where Vilette, who was a lawyer, conducted his business. But how many Western lawyers have a bead curtain across the doorway to their studies? Bead curtains are common in countries with hot climates, but otherwise the establishments in which one is most likely to find one in a non-period movie tend to be sleazy, such as the strip joint or the seedy bar (bead curtains occur in both these sorts of premises in, for example, *Touch of Evil* [Orson Welles,

1958]) or indeed the brothel, e.g., the room of Iris (Jodie Foster) in *Taxi Driver* (Martin Scorsese, 1976). The bead curtain at the back of the Bunne Shoppe in *Downhill* marks very precisely the entrance to the darkened, sensual area where Mabel (Annette Benson) effects her seduction. But, apart from *I Confess*, the only other example I can recall of a bead curtain in a private house is in Geiger's house in *The Big Sleep* (Howard Hawks, 1946), and in that case there is no doubt that the curtain is contributing to the general seediness of the premises, which are associated with all kinds of "deviant" behavior.[13] I am therefore assuming that the bead curtain in *I Confess* is a code: a way of hinting that this was the sort of house where rather dubious goings-on occurred, probably of a sexual nature.

Although such speculations refer to issues which are outside the scope of this essay, I would like to note one intimation regarding the swaying curtain: it suggests that the murderer has just disappeared "off-stage." William Rothman has written that "In Hitchcock, when the curtain opens, theater is invoked."[14] One might indeed argue that Hitchcock's use of curtains in general is almost always theatrical, as in the examples of the concealed guns in *Saboteur* and *The Man Who Knew Too Much*. I would suggest therefore that both the row of empty chairs and the curtain in the opening scene of *I Confess* evoke a sense of theater. It's as if the camera has craned in to Vilette's study at the end of a "performance" — which we have just missed.

As Keller escapes down the street, we see that he is wearing a cassock, which he quickly removes (he wore a costume for the "performance"). Shortly afterwards, he confesses to Father Logan that he has killed Vilette. Later in the film, it is established that the murder also impinges on Logan's personal life. Vilette had been blackmailing Ruth about her past relationship with Logan. Moreover, on the night of the murder, Logan had promised Ruth that he would "deal with" Vilette.

It is not difficult to see that the relationship between Logan and Keller echoes that between Guy and Bruno in

Strangers on a Train. Just as Bruno kills Guy's wife Miriam (Laura Elliott) "for" Guy, so it's as if Keller has killed Vilette "for" Logan. It is true that, in *I Confess*, the killer does not know that the murder of this particular person "solves" the hero's problem. Nevertheless, structurally Keller is like Bruno: the hero's demonic double, carrying out the crime that the hero—albeit, in Logan's case, unconsciously—wants. This "perverse" connection haunts their relationship all the way through to the final scene.

In the hotel ballroom at the end, there are elements which specifically echo those in the opening scene. Again there are chairs along the walls: in this case, along the whole length of each side of the ballroom. And again there is a curtain, albeit a conventional one: it's at the back of the stage. After shooting at the first two policemen who arrive at the entrance to the ballroom, Keller opens this curtain to see if there is a way out through it, and, surprisingly, there isn't. We might remember that, when similarly seeking to escape, Jordan heads towards the curtain at the back of the stage in *The 39 Steps*, policemen pour through it. But in Keller's case, all the exits are physically closed.

I am arguing that this whole scene functions structurally as an "answer" to the unseen drama in Vilette's study which culminated in murder. Zupančič's explanation for the use of the ballroom for the *dénouement* focuses on its spatial contrast with the confessional in which Keller confesses to Logan. As the stage is "the public setting *par excellence*, where everything that is said is intended for the audience" (81), it serves as an ideal location to release the secret divulged in the confessional. I find this argument only partly convincing. It seems to me much more striking that the murderer's final confrontation with the law—and his confession—are played out in an arena in which the suggestive theatrical elements in the opening scene have, as in a dream displacement, been expanded and incorporated into a "genuine" theatrical space. On the stage and then beside it, Keller is presented as giving a performance—the murderer defying the law—to those watching him from just outside the ballroom entrance, including Larrue and Logan. Hitchcock reinforces this by filming Keller only from the entrance, approximating the point of view of the group just outside. But it is the material of the murder scene that is being evoked. At the moment when Larrue shouts "What about Vilette?," Keller is clambering over the row of chairs, looking to see if there is a way out through the window, a combination of elements which specifically evokes Vilette's study. (Given that Keller, by his own account, was wearing a cassock "to avoid attention," it is hard to imagine that he entered Vilette's study through the window, which he then left open. Nevertheless, I assume, with Deborah Thomas, that that is what we are *supposed* to think.[15])

Larrue's shouted question is the equivalent of Hannay's shouted "What are the 39 steps?," and it similarly prompts Keller to "confess." As with Mr. Memory, this is a confession only by implication: Keller assumes that Logan has broken his vows and talked, and so there is no point now in denying that he himself is Vilette's murderer. Instead, he vilifies Logan, calling him a coward and a hypocrite.

As Keller is doing this, those just outside the ballroom—now also including Father Millais, Ruth, and her husband Pierre (Roger Dann)—register the implications: that Logan had been unable to talk because he had heard the truth from Keller in confession. And so, for all these people, Logan is now not only innocent, but honorable, faithful to his vocation. But Logan looks highly distressed during Keller's outburst, and we can see why. Keller himself thinks that Logan has betrayed him. By filming Keller up to this point only in distance shots, Hitchcock has stressed the expanse of the ballroom floor between him and the group at the entrance. It is my contention that Logan, upset that Keller thinks so badly of him, now finds this distance between Keller and himself unbearable. And so, as a police marksman shoots and wounds Keller, Logan breaks away from the group, enters the ballroom, and begins to walk across the floor towards Keller. He wants to talk to him.

It should be obvious that the ballroom setting and the scene overall are not like the other theatrical climaxes in

Hitchcock: no excited audience, no shots from the villain's point of view of the blocked exits, no high angle "spotlight" shots of the villain; in other words, none of the rhetoric of the paranoid structure. As I have indicated, there are theatrical elements to the scene, but they are different, and are deployed differently. Apart from the stage and its proscenium arch, the feature to which Hitchcock gives most prominence throughout the scene is the space across the ballroom floor. But the scene cannot be brought to a resolution until this space is eliminated. Logan has to get close to Keller.

As Logan walks towards Keller, Hitchcock films this with his familiar track-and-reverse point-of-view editing, crosscutting between a track forward showing Logan's point of view of Keller getting closer, and a reverse angle track back in front of Logan. I have suggested elsewhere that Hitchcock uses this technique when he wishes us to identify with a character's apprehension about what he or she is headed towards.[16] That Logan would feel apprehension here is self-evident: Keller has been shooting at anything he thinks is a threat. Indeed, he says he will shoot Logan. However, as Logan gets closer, their interaction in fact becomes more intimate. Logan calls Keller "Otto" for the first time in the film, and, as V.F. Perkins has pointed out, "It turns out that Keller can kill his wife . . . but not the priest."[17] Nevertheless, Keller is still blaming Logan, saying that it is his fault that Alma is dead. He then seeks to project his own loneliness onto the priest, before provoking the police to shoot him again by pretending to shoot at Logan. Begging Logan's forgiveness, he then dies in his arms.

The police bullets here are in effect the superego punishment of the villain. The first is intended to disarm a dangerous killer, but, like Jordan shooting Mr. Memory, it also brutally halts a performance. Again, the shooting occurs immediately after "the confession," as though the superego cannot wait to act. As soon as a villain is identified and exposed "on stage," retribution swiftly follows.

For all the theatrical elements of this *dénouement*, it seems entirely fitting that it ends—and the film ends—with an intimate close-up of Logan holding Keller. It's as though Logan here is in some sense finally accepting his murderous alter ego as a part of himself. As Keller is dying, he can genuinely embrace him. (Although Guy does not actually embrace Bruno, the penultimate scene of *Strangers on a Train* is similar.) It is also important that two distinct types of superego figure are present, each implicitly bestowing approval: Larrue to signal that the law is satisfied, and that Logan has been cleared of the taint of murder, and Father Millais to signal that the Church is satisfied, and that it was only because Logan was true to his vocation that he had become so plausible a suspect.

The theatrical elements here are thus dissolved by the end of the scene. Once the police have halted the "performance," the dynamic of the scene shifts to the interaction between Logan and Keller. Nevertheless, that Hitchcock has set this whole scene in a theatrical space emphasizes the importance of such settings in his work. It is well known that he is drawn to certain sorts of setting for his climaxes and *dénouements*: in particular, famous landmarks and locations with crowds. The theater and equivalent settings should also be included: there is something about the arena of a theater that lends itself to a dramatic set piece, even when, as in *I Confess*, he uses the space in a rather different way.

The Theater Death Scene in Non-Hitchcock Films

In order to get a clearer sense of Hitchcock's distinctive use of the theater death scene, I would like to look briefly at other film examples of this type of scene. There is, in fact, a crucial real-life incident which is relevant here: the assassination of President Lincoln by John Wilkes Booth in Ford's Theater, Washington, D.C., in 1865. This has been dramatized on film many times, most famously in *The Birth of a Nation* (D.W. Griffith, 1915). And the material of this assassination scene can be seen to lie behind a number of the subsequent theater death scenes in films. For example, Lincoln was shot in his box, dramatically interrupting an onstage theatrical performance, and Booth then leapt from the box onto the stage—as in *The 39 Steps*. An early theater death scene that almost certainly influenced Hitchcock occurs at the end of *Spione* (Fritz Lang, 1928). The villain Haghi (Rudolf Klein-Rogge), a double agent, is cornered on stage during a performance: first, he notices policemen in the orchestra pit pointing guns at him; then he sees the hero, the heroine, and the chief spymaster (a superego figure) watching him from the wings. He fires at these three, but then sees that men with guns are also waiting in the wings. Realizing that there is no way out, he shoots himself. The scene provides a highly dramatic ending to the film: before he dies, Haghi calls "Curtain!" and the last shot is of the audience applauding as the curtain closes. Lang shoots from Haghi's point of view to capture his sense of being trapped, and so here we do indeed have an example of the "paranoid structure" so central to the Hitchcock examples. In particular, the stage death here is turned into a spectacle, a spectacle which in this case the audience ironically appreciates.

Nevertheless, it was above all *The 39 Steps* which popularized the theater death scene. I would like to look at four of the major subsequent non-Hitchcock examples,[18] and consider the extent to which they, too, conform to Zupančič's three basic criteria: confrontation with the representatives of the law, admission of guilt, and punishment. This will enable the specificity of the Hitchcock versions of the scene to be clarified.

At the climax of *Seven Sinners* (Albert de Courville, 1936)—scripted by Sidney Gilliat and Frank Launder, future scriptwriters of *The Lady Vanishes* (1938)—the hero John Harwood (Edmund Lowe) catches up with the villain Turbé (Thomy Bourdelle) in a newsreel theater (a cinema). The newsreel on screen is showing the series of train wrecks for which Turbé is responsible, and it is evident that Turbé has come to see it in order to gloat over his work. As Harwood identifies himself to Turbé, he signals to the police in the cinema that this is the man they are seeking. Turbé tries to make a break for it, a fight with the police ensues, and the audience panics. Mounting the stage, Turbé shoots at Harwood, and is then himself shot by a policeman. Throughout this, the newsreel has continued, its voiceover discussing the train wrecks. As Harwood and the heroine Caryl (Constance Cummings) now look at the body of Turbé, the voiceover wonders: "Who is the insane criminal responsible for these most ghastly crimes of our century?" Cut to Turbé's body, lying on the stage beneath the newsreel images: "When and how will he be brought to justice?"

In this case, all three of Zupančič's features are present. However, the essence of the Hitchcock paradigm—the wrong man structure, and the scene as a public corrective to the misperception of the hero as guilty—does not apply; as in *Spione*, there is no falsely-accused figure. Instead, the scene makes an ingenious link between the crimes of the master villain and his death, suggesting hubris: he is caught because he wanted to savor his malevolent power. Nevertheless, also as in *Spione*, he is shot on the stage, so that the sense of the stage as dangerous (to a man) is the same as in the Hitchcock films.

In *The Return of Frank James* (Fritz Lang, 1940), the killers of Jesse James are performing in a theatrical version of the killing—which rewrites them as heroes, saving a woman from being robbed by Jesse and his brother Frank—when they are confronted by Frank himself (Henry Fonda), glowering at them from a box over the stage. No one is killed, but the villains are dramatically exposed on stage, and they start a fire in the theater in order to escape from the vengeful wrath of Frank, here the superego figure, who leaps onto the stage in order to pursue them. Although this scene would seem to refer only obliquely to Zupančič's features, it nevertheless conforms to them at a deeper level: the play distorts the truth, but Frank's presence confronts the villains with their distortion, and their terrified flight from him is like an admission of guilt.

The Lodger (John Brahm, 1944) is a Hollywood version of Marie Belloc Lowndes's novel which, unlike Hitchcock's, follows the novel in making the Lodger, Slade (Laird Cregar), "Jack the Ripper" (the film is set in London in 1889). The climax, however, seems like a reworking of that of *The 39 Steps*. Here the heroine, Kitty (Merle Oberon), a dancer, is on stage, Slade is in the audience, and the hero, Inspector John Warwick (George Sanders), a Scotland Yard detective, is among the policemen searching the theater to capture Slade. This sets up a different dynamic to the scene. Goaded into a frenzy of puritanical repression by Kitty's suggestive Parisian dance, Slade slips past the police and assaults her in her dressing-room. Her screams bring Warwick and the police racing to her rescue, and the news that Jack the Ripper is in the theater panics the audience into fleeing out into the street. After an extended chase through the theater, during which Slade contrives another attempt on Kitty's life, the police eventually corner him at the back of the theater, and he jumps through a window to drown in the River Thames.

For the first time in these examples, it is a woman on stage who triggers the disturbance, albeit in the mind of a psychotic man. This in turn highlights the crucial absence of such a source of disturbance in the Hitchcock examples. Nevertheless, apart from the displacement away from the stage for the final confrontation, the sequence fits Zupančič's criteria fairly closely. Once again, a theater has proved an excellent setting in which to draw together the different threads of the plot into a dramatic climax.

My final example has a different provenance. The theater climax of *The Godfather Part III* (Francis Ford Coppola, 1990) is certainly indebted to Hitchcock, but it is the Albert Hall sequence in *The Man Who Knew Too Much* (1955) which is invoked. The sequence involves an assassination attempt on Michael Corleone (Al Pacino), the gangster hero, during a performance of Mascagni's opera *Cavalleria Rusticana*. As the assassin, Mosca (Mario Donatone), disguised as a priest, moves into position to shoot from box to box across the stalls, there are many felicitous details which echo the Hitchcock sequence. In fact, Mosca is frustrated in his attempt to shoot Michael in the theater itself, but, as the Corleone family is leaving at the end of the performance, he carries it out on the steps of the theater. It is here that the "theater death scene" is enacted, but Coppola raises it to another level by staging it not simply as theater but as an operatic climax. This applies both to the tragic outcome of the scene and to the heightened rhetoric of its style. The person who is actually killed in the shooting is not the corrupt hero, but his innocent teenage daughter Mary (Sofia Coppola), and her death produces paroxysms of grief from her bereaved parents. Here the guilt of the "villain," so crucial to a number of the Hitchcock theater scenes, combines with the shock of the loss to produce in Michael a histrionic scream of agony. This powerful climax demonstrates that there is yet another major inspirational source for theater death scenes: the opera.

Conclusion

I have noted the details of the non-Hitchcock theater death scenes in order to make two general points. First, that only Hitchcock has used the scene so extensively, and elaborated it through so many permutations. Second, and more importantly, that, from *Spione* onwards—and with the obvious exception of *The Godfather Part III*—almost all of the non-Hitchcock examples also fit Zupančič's three basic criteria. There are occasional variations, such as the villains escaping in *The Return of Frank James*, but in general the Zupančič elements are present. This also applies to most of the scenes I mention in note 18. It is not until the additional features of the "theater climax paradigm" are included that one can discern the parameters of a peculiarly Hitchcockian theater death scene. His distinctive touch is found in the details which Zupančič does not consider: that these scenes (1) occur in the falsely-accused man (or woman) films, and the public exposé of the villain serves in effect to counteract the public perception of the hero/heroine as guilty; (2) include a mobilization of an array of superego figures, not just the police, who mete out "justice" to the villain and clear the falsely-accused hero of wrongdoing; and (3) deploy a corpus of rhetorical devices, including spotlights, spotlight shots, and point-of-view shots of those who threaten the villain on the stage, all of which combine to create a "paranoid structure" around him. Structurally, these additional features mesh with and enrich Zupančič's basic ingredients. But they also reveal the specifics of the *Hitchcock* theater death scene. Only *Spione* stands out as in some respects comparable.

Nevertheless, behind these elements there still remains the question, "Why should the stage setting seem so dangerous for men in Hitchcock's films?" I would like to begin to answer this by looking at the sort of men who frequent the stage, many of whom are villains. The notion that a villain, who necessarily has something to hide, should be at home in the masquerade of the theater applies to Fane, Mr. Memory, and Guy in *Young and Innocent* (hence the relevance of the blackface "disguise"). Among the non-Hitchcock examples, it applies similarly to the villains in both the Lang films as well as to someone like Anthony John (Ronald Colman) in *A Double Life* (George Cukor, 1948), a psychotic killer who is unmasked on stage while playing Othello in blackface. It is on stage, while enacting an "official" masquerade, that the false masquerade of the criminal is revealed. In this context, it is worth noting the real-life case of John Wilkes Booth, who was by profession an actor. In leaping onto the stage, he also presented himself to the public as Lincoln's assassin, even declaiming "Sic semper tyrannis!" — presumably with a theatrical flourish. In front of an audience, he unmasked himself.

However, being on stage also involves being looked at, which tends to disturb Hitchcock's men. With women, it is different. There is no problem about them being on stage, displaying themselves: this does not threaten gender norms. But when Hitchcock's men are on stage, a paranoid structure tends to come into play: a sense that one is being subjected to an accusatory, threatening collective gaze. This is particularly true when the police or other "representatives of the law" make an appearance. Being on stage heightens the fear, which so many of Hitchcock's men possess, of being subjected to the gaze and hence objectified.

The theater climaxes in Hitchcock show extreme, indeed violent, examples of this. In Freudian terms, these scenes are "overdetermined," the product of a condensation of elements. And one effect is that the villains on stage are psychically "ripped bare": with no place to run, they are shot, executed, driven crazy. Moreover, on a number of occasions this happens in public, thereby exacerbating the villain's humiliation.

Behind this violence lie the demands of a punitive superego. The villain has been identified, caught in the gaze of the superego figure(s), at which point he is peremptorily punished. That this punishment almost invariably involves a violent death—a feature which applies just as readily to the non-Hitchcock examples—is a reflection of the conventions of popular filmmaking, specifically Hollywood filmmaking. In *The Movies*, Richard Griffith and Arthur Mayer quote from advice which Herman Mankiewicz gave to Ben Hecht when the latter arrived in Hollywood in the late 1920s. In a Hollywood movie, Mankiewicz insisted, the villain must, finally, be shot.[19] I assume that he would have been happy for the villain to be killed by other means, but the point he was making was basic to Hollywood: it is simply more satisfactory for an audience that the villain be killed, rather than merely arrested, at the end of a movie.

The theater is a suitable place to die in these movies because it is also a suitable place to stage the climactic set piece, which will, very often, include the unmasking and then the death of the villain. But behind this lie many other Hitchcock features and elements, the most important of which is that these deaths all concern men, and that women on stage generate a very different dynamic. On stage is female space, and men venture there at their peril.

Notes

This article is an expanded version of a paper delivered at a symposium, "The Wrong Artist: Hitchcock and the Other Arts" held at MuHKA Media, Antwerp, Belgium in November 2007. I am very grateful to Steven Jacobs and the staff at the media center for the opportunity to speak at the symposium. Many thanks as always to Leighton Grist for very productive feedback during the drafting of the article, and to Richard Allen and Sidney Gottlieb for equally constructive editorial suggestions.

1. Jane E. Sloan, *Alfred Hitchcock: A Definitive Filmography* (Berkeley and Los Angeles: University of California Press, 1995), 612.

2. Alenka Zupančič, "A Perfect Place to Die: Theater in Hitchcock's Films," in Slavoj Žižek, ed., *Everything You Always Wanted to Know about Lacan (But Were Afraid to Ask Hitchcock)* (London: Verso, 1992), 73-105. Further quotations from this essay are cited in the text of my essay by page number only.

3. Michael Walker, "Hitchcockian Narrative: A Provisional Model," *Hitchcock Annual* 15 (2006-07): 122-63, especially 160-61.

4. Unfortunately, Zupančič makes an alarming number of mistakes in her description of what happens in the theater at the end of *Stage Fright*; see "A Perfect Place to Die," 80.

5. There is a similar sense of theater to the courtroom sequence in *The Manxman* (1929).

6. Margaret M. Horwitz, "*The Birds*: A Mother's Love," in Marshall Deutelbaum and Leland Poague, eds., *A Hitchcock Reader* (Ames, Iowa: Iowa State University Press, 1986), 281.

7. Walker, "Hitchcockian Narrative," 149.

8. Sabrina Barton, "'Criss-Cross': Paranoia and Projection in *Strangers on a Train*," *Camera Obscura* 25-26 (1991): 75-100.

9. Although Lang creates a similar effect in *M* (1931), it isn't the same. When Beckert (Peter Lorre) realizes that he is being tailed, Lang only briefly uses point-of-view shots; he is more concerned with the shifting nature of the trap Beckert finds himself in. The dominant metaphor here is of a hunted animal, and when Beckert is finally apprehended and "imprisoned" in the beam of a torchlight by the criminals, Lang suggests a terrified animal trapped in the headlights of a car. Nevertheless, one cannot deny that Lang was an influence on Hitchcock, and I return to this briefly later.

10. I refer to Michael's killing of Gromek (Wolfgang Kieling) as murder because I don't think that Gromek intends to kill Michael, simply arrest him.

11. See Richard Allen, "Sir John and the Half-Caste: Identity and Representation in Hitchcock's *Murder!*," *Hitchcock Annual* 13 (2004-05): 92-126.

12. Ina Rae Hark, "Keeping Your Amateur Standing: Audience Participation and Good Citizenship in Hitchcock's Political Films," *Cinema Journal* 29, no. 2 (1990), 8.

13. Michael Walker, "*The Big Sleep*: Howard Hawks and Film Noir," in Ian Cameron, ed., *The Movie Book of Film Noir* (London: Studio Vista, 1992); published in the U.S. as *The Book of Film Noir* (New York: Continuum, 1993), 191-202; see especially 195-98.

14. William Rothman, *Hitchcock—The Murderous Gaze* (Cambridge: Harvard University Press, 1986), 298.

15. Deborah Thomas, "Confession as Betrayal: Hitchcock's *I Confess* as Enigmatic Text," *CineAction* 40 (May 1996), 36.

16. Michael Walker, "The Stolen Raincoat and the Bloodstained Dress: *Young and Innocent* and *Stage Fright*," in Richard Allen and S. Ishii-Gonzalès, eds., *Alfred Hitchcock Centenary Essays* (London: BFI, 1999), 197.

17. V.F. Perkins, "*I Confess*: Photographs of People Speaking," *CineAction* 52 (June 2000), 39.

18. Other films with theater death scenes include *The Westerner* (William Wyler, 1940), *To Be or Not To Be* (Ernst Lubitsch, 1942), *Charade* (Stanley Donen, 1963), and *Phantom of the Paradise* (Brian de Palma, 1974). In addition, *Scaramouche* (George Sidney, 1952) includes a superb example of such a scene, but without a death.

19. Richard Griffith and Arthur Mayer, *The Movies*, second ed. (London: Hamlyn, 1971), 64.

JAMES M. VEST

Reflections on the Making of To Catch a Thief: André Bazin, Sylvette Baudrot, Grace Kelly, Charles Vanel, and Brigitte Auber

Introduction

Location filming for To Catch a Thief was scheduled for the French Riviera and the nearby hill country in the Maritime Alps from late May through June 1954. However, unsettled weather and other problems impeded production, and second-unit photography continued there for several weeks after Hitchcock and his cast returned to California.[1] The challenges of the French shoot were memorable to participants and observers alike, some of whom recorded contemporaneous accounts of their experiences that summer, while others recounted their recollections after the release of the film in 1955.

Among the former was Sylvette Baudrot, "la script-girl" and occasional translator for Hitchcock's French-speaking visitors. In a distinguished career spanning a half century, Baudrot would supervise scripts and assure continuity on over sixty films, including Jacques Tati's Mon Oncle (1958) and Playtime (1967), Alain Resnais' Hiroshima mon amour (1959) and Last Year at Marienbad (1961), Louis Malle's Zazie dans le métro (1960) and Lacombe Lucien (1974), Roman Polanski's The Pianist (2002) and Oliver Twist (2005), and Julian Schnabel's The Diving Bell and the Butterfly (2007). Baudrot's diary entries for To Catch a Thief are lively verbal sketches that provide an insider's perspective on the director and his working methods, including his interest in ambient sounds at certain hours of the night, the number of times he actually looked through the viewfinder, his combative perspective on censorship, and his curiosity about French soufflés. Her musings call attention to the subtle movements of his hands and to his "unsettlingly palpable" presence even when physically absent. As published in *Cahiers du Cinéma*, Baudrot's reflections also illuminate the jocular but sometimes tense relationship between Hitchcock and the dean of European cinema critics, André Bazin.

In July 1954, the redoubtable Bazin, co-founder and co-editor of *Cahiers*, was responsible for writing the magazine's "Cinema Diary" column. That assignment, which rotated among staff members, involved day-by-day reflections on unfolding events relating to cinema. This was challenging for Bazin while he was vacationing with his family in the Provençal village of Tourettes-sur-Loup, far from the main sites of film production and at some distance from the nearest movie house. That situation changed radically, however, when a film crew from Paramount came to Tourettes and the picturesque village became the setting for a vehicular chase in *To Catch a Thief*. Beginning with ruminations on the history of location filming in this remote area of southeastern France, Bazin's journal entries included dynamic accounts of his contacts with a noisy helicopter used for aerial filming and other technical aspects of that shoot in the summer of 1954. The conjunction of the traditional and the modern became a leitmotif in these informal, highly personal reflections on the intersection of art and life—of bulky moviemaking equipment amid flocks of sheep and fragrant flowers— recorded by Bazin over the course of several thought-provoking days. In the process, one of the fiercest European critics of Hitchcock's work entrusted to the future, through these diary entries, a side of himself rarely seen and glimmers of a significant transition in his thinking about this director's techniques, aims, and art.

As part of his ongoing research on Hitchcock's films, Bruno Villien, frequent contributor to *Le Nouvel Observateur* and *Opéra*, interviewed actors who played major roles in *To Catch a Thief*. Villien included their statements in his 1982 book, *Hitchcock*, which is yet to be translated into English. His interviewees were Brigitte Auber, the young gymnast and aspiring actress who played the kittenish Danielle Foussard; Charles Vanel, the veteran actor known for his roles in suspenseful films of Henri-Georges Clouzot (*Wages of Fear* [1953], *Diaboliques* [1955]), here cast as the complicitous restaurateur, Augustus Bertani; and the film's female lead, identified by Villien as "la Princesse Grace de Monaco." All three performers provided glimpses into Hitchcock's character and habits, while supplying pertinent details about his conduct during his sojourn in France. Together their commentaries offer a distinctive portrait of Hitchcock the director, the caustic Francophile, the art collector, the epicure, the gamester.

The selections that follow represent a variety of perspectives and *partis pris* from actors, a crew member, and a major critic. They offer unique glimpses of the director's working methods, as they attest to his personal and professional impact on those around him. Previously unavailable in English, they provide fresh insights into the making of a film that, although sometimes viewed as a minor *divertissement*, significantly altered the course of French film criticism, helped relaunch the international career of "le grand Alfred," and led to the first book-length study of his work by Eric Rohmer and Claude Chabrol and to his extensive, revelatory interviews with François Truffaut and other cinephiles.[2]

Day to Day with Hitch:
Diary Entries

by Sylvette Baudrot[3]

On the plane, May 1954
Delighted to be going to the Riviera to begin a new film. Also curious to get to know the director, Alfred Hitchcock, but

cautiously curious because this gentleman has quite a reputation as one of the greatest of American directors, as the master of suspense. No clue as to his physical appearance, his habits; I can't recall having ever seen his picture. A little anxious, basically, about working with him.

4th day of filming
Haven't seen A. Hitchcock since my arrival. The only thing I've seen of him are some sketches, which had the force of orders,[4] along with the crew members' script for exterior shots. His assistant imposes the will of the boss: Hitch wants this or that done just so. Despite his absence, the director's presence is unsettlingly palpable.

5th day
Clouds. We wait. A Chrysler parks near the filming site. Inside the Chrysler, a cigar. One by one the principal crew members and actors speak through the car's open window. During lunch a shadowy figure remains inside. Hitchcock never lunches (because of his weight) and reads instead. Still no sun. The Chrysler takes off before I can make out anything more than a plump fellow exhaling curls of cigar smoke. The great director: undeniably very distant!

6th day
Hitchcock chats with the crew. This fellow never stops telling stories, making jokes, talking about the characters in the film, jumping from one subject to another with absolute freedom. With Cary Grant he complains about the attraction of French food: "I'm going to get fat if this continues. You young people have all sorts of ways to lose weight. But me, with my monastic lifestyle!..."[5]
Nevertheless he possesses a fine ear and great attention to detail. Earlier I talked with Cary Grant about his shirt—too American in my opinion, although apparently bought in France. Shortly thereafter C. Grant came back wearing a pullover. To my astonishment he told me that Hitch, who had overheard everything, had asked him to change.

"Do you like the fireworks sequence?" Hitchcock asked me. "American censors forced me to change the ending." To the censors those fireworks, which serve as counterpoint to the evolving relationship between the protagonists, appeared too crude, and some maneuvering was necessary. Hitch delights in besting the censors.[6] In that context he recounted to me the story of his latest film, *Rear Window*, about which the censors also protested loudly. He prefers that film with its mix of suspense, humor, and details of everyday life to all the others he's made in the United States (a judgment seemingly not shared by viewers at the Venice Film Festival).

The weather remains chancy. We were unable to film a sequence on a terrace overlooking Saint-Jeannet.[7] Hitch does not shilly-shally. He has been producer on his films for some time. He makes a decision: two days' delay is too much. Backgrounds will be filmed for transparencies and the set will be reconstructed in Hollywood. Afterwards, for other sequences, Hitch will film only the location shots that involve the [principal] actors, then closeups will be made in the studio. Hitch does not like to waste time.

Saint-Cézaire[8]

For once the legend is justified: Hitch almost never looks through the camera. His indications are sufficiently precise and the cameraman so faithful that he has no need to verify [each set-up]. During the making of this film Hitch looked through the viewfinder three times, when his director of photography declared that, since they could not control the course of the sun, they would need to change the placement of the camera. Hitch did not become upset and immediately found another position suitable to the changing light.

Cannes

Hitch invited me to dinner. He asked me to translate the recipe for a raspberry soufflé that had made a big impression on him. A month later, in the body of a long telegram that he sent us from the States, giving instructions for filming transparencies, this phrase [appeared]: "Ask Sylvette whether the grated cheese should be blended into the egg whites or mixed with the other ingredients..." Hitch was having problems with his culinary experiments.

High Corniche[9]
    A crane maneuvers a powerful motor car into place, carefully balanced on the edge of the road just above the cliff. Hitch often evokes impossibilities, improbable scenes, tricks that he delights in creating in his films; for example, a scene viewed through a monocle or an airplane crashing into the sea, accomplished with tons of water breaking through the transparency screen, etc....
    Hitch [usually] has his hands crossed over his belly in an attitude of waiting or reflection, except when he walks around, stiff as a post, stretching to full height with his arms dancing about. When he enters into discussion his right hand holds the fingers of his left, except for the index finger, which is pointed toward the ground. At other times, from early morning on, he may be seen smoking a cigar.

Cannes
    Hitch remains perfectly relaxed during filming. He has a profound sense of what he wants his finished film to look like. There is no need for him to look at the script.
    He asked me to serve as interpreter for an interview [with André Bazin in Nice] during the set-up for a shot. At the end of the session [Hitchcock remarked] to Bazin, who had apologized for taking him away from filming, "Do you think I would have stayed if I were wasting my time?"[10] I'll leave it to Bazin himself to recount the conclusion to his second encounter with Hitchcock.[11]

Cannes, July
    Hitch has left to continue interior shooting in Hollywood. He gave me a list of over fifty sounds to record, including:
    — ambient noises on the Croisette [Promenade at Cannes], at eleven P.M.
    — same, at two in the morning

— same, at four in the morning
etc....
Now Hitch corrects the shooting of transparencies by telegram. Every day, [he sends] a long message [such as this one]:

Dear Herbie (his American assistant director [Herbert Coleman]). Viewed shot where car barely misses oncoming bus. Afraid that does not work for following reasons: because we, the camera, taking a curve, see bus so suddenly that it has already passed before we realize danger. Thinking of two corrections to make. First, we should extend the long straight road shot with curve in distance so as to be aware of the curve well before getting to it. When we get to the curve, we should then be shocked to discover the bus coming straight at us, because, the curve being narrow, the bus must travel on the left, but we the camera must never take the curve. Second, in projection only half the bus appears on the screen. I realize this is due to your swerving to miss it. That can be remedied by keeping the camera aimed well to the left, so that at the same time the traveling shot from the car approaches the turn, the camera pans from left to right. All the other shots are of breathtaking beauty. Best wishes to the whole team. And especially to Sylvette. — Hitch[12]

I hope the memories we have given Alfred Hitchcock are equal to those we retain of Hitch: a great fellow, a very personal director, but also a friend who allowed us to collaborate with him on his film.

The Little Cinema Diary (from Tourettes-sur-Loup) [excerpts]

by André Bazin[13]

3 July
Doniol-Valcroze wrote to say that it was my turn to do the "Little Cinema Diary" column [for the next issue of *Cahiers*].[14]

But where am I going to find cinema at Tourettes-sur-Loup? The regional film club circuit that on Tuesday evenings brings to the Café Cresp 16mm versions of inaudible Italian melodramas will not suffice. Let's address the problem from another angle. Cinema encompasses those who make it and those who write about it. So if Saint-Paul-de-Vence is the mecca for filmmakers, Tourettes seems, more modestly nestled among its violets, the refuge of film critics. I would include among them, even though they might not apply that label to themselves, in addition to your servant and co-editor of this magazine, François Timmory, former managing editor of *L'Ecran Français* and Robert Chazal, former editor of *Cinémonde*.[15]

I might also evoke the cinematographic past of Tourettes, but a single issue of *Cahiers* would not suffice for that task. In terms of backdrops or sites of greater or lesser importance to the action, Tourettes-sur-Loup has figured in an astounding number of films, among them *Les Visiteurs du soir, La Guerre des boutons, La Route Napoléon, Juliette ou la clé des songes, Ernest le Rebelle, Les Gueux au paradis*, etc. That list is far from complete, and I discovered, by questioning "old locals," that films have been made at Tourettes since, and perhaps even before, the First World War. . . .

4 July
The tradition continues. Once again this morning the helicopter for *To Catch a Thief* is roaring above Tourettes. For a month Hitchcock—comfortably ensconced at the Carlton Hotel in Cannes—was filming in picturesque sites around this area. This will certainly be a compendium of Provençal tourist attractions. He has been everywhere: in the charming little terraced cemetery at Cagnes, on the highway near Gréolières, in the flower market at Nice, on the beach at the Carlton.[16] Hitchcock took off for Hollywood a few days ago, but he left a second-unit crew here to assure continuity of exterior shots. That explains why the helicopter is still around. It's for a chase sequence involving a black, front-wheel drive police car and a shiny, reddish Delahaye sports car, which must certainly

contain gangsters.[17] They pass through the village and the police vehicle is blocked on the far side by a flock of sheep. The helicopter records the chase from the air. It must come from London, helicopters being rare in France since Dien-Bien-Phu. It's based in a field a hundred yards from my window. All the local youngsters gather around it, held back by a rope. Untiringly, the chopper rises, slips out over the valley, follows the sinuous highway, then returns to its resting place. Surely it is staking out the route and camera angles needed for refilming the chase. That seems laborious, monotonous. Even the kids become indifferent to the routine long before the helicopter makes its last pass of the day. Traffic is stopped for 500 yards by police officers on motorcycles and technicians, chatting confidentially with the sky on their walkie-talkies. On the hillside the sheep and their owner wait patiently in the shade. A newborn lamb trembles on uncertain legs near its mother. The routine continues until evening....

5 July
Again, the helicopter. See yesterday's entry.

6 July
Ditto. That cursed sequence is showing signs of stress. It seems that the helicopter is encountering strong wind gusts and the instability makes photography very difficult.

7 July
So much for the helicopter and its pilot. We're taking off for Arles, by way of the Saint-Raphaël Film Festival, with our son and pet parrot in tow. . . .

12 July
Return to Tourettes. . . .

13 July
I learn that the helicopter did not go back to London until day before yesterday. That sequence must have been expensive!

15 July
    Cinema is still at Tourettes. The crew of *To Catch a Thief*
has returned and built a huge steel platform beside the
highway in hopes of establishing continuity with the aerial
shots. Hitchcock, who from Hollywood envisions shooting
plans three days in advance, cabled that [in previously shot
footage] one could not feel strongly enough the vehicles'
emergence from the village. The thirty-foot-high platform will
allow for a better intermediary shot. Chatting with the French
technicians, I learn that from a distance of about 6,000 miles
this devil of a man gives them the impression of keeping close
watch over their work almost as if he were here. Worse still, in
his absence there is no way to avoid executing his plan.[18] This
shot confirms my opinion, garnered from other conversations
with Hitchcock or those who work with him, namely that in
every shot one should *feel* something. The search for this
tension, for this "internal becoming" of the shot that
transcends the dramatic event itself, may be the key to
Hitchcock's *mise-en-scène*. If, in an editing room in Hollywood,
Hitchcock should discover that one did not "feel" the cars
leaving the village, then [at his command] everything here
must begin anew. . . .

"La Main au Collet [*To Catch a Thief*]"
— from Bruno Villien, *Hitchcock*[19]

Grace Kelly

    "Hitchcock may live in America," said Princess Grace,
"but he is still very British in his habits. He is also French on
the side—his gourmet side. He adores French food and
French wines! While we were working on *To Catch a Thief*, and
even earlier, during the making of *Rear Window*, Hitchcock
was on a diet. He wanted ten pounds 'to play with,' that he
could gain back while dining superbly in France! When he
arrived in France, he allowed three days for the [normally
one-day] trip from Paris to Cannes, stopping at renowned
restaurants along the way. He wanted me to do likewise and

arranged for me to follow the same itinerary. But I was working on another film and unfortunately the intervening time was too brief. We started filming at Cannes and on the Riviera in June. Then we returned to California for the interior shots. The exterior shooting, which is always more difficult, was further complicated by bad weather. There was a lot of rain....

"This role was unusual, quite comic: Frances is very different from other characters [I've played]. As for costumes, Hitchcock gave me complete freedom with Edith Head. She and I had a great time doing whatever we liked, except for the gown for the costume ball. Hitchcock had a definite idea: he wanted it totally gold! But aside from that he left me free to choose as I pleased.

"As for the picnic scene, we filmed the beginning in Monaco, but the closeups of Cary Grant and me were filmed in the studio with rear projection. For the chase scenes, when it was a long shot, it was a stunt woman driving, except in those shots where you could recognize me. Cary Grant was concerned because I'm very nearsighted. I had to drive that powerful sports car and stop it in a little thicket right at the edge of the Middle Corniche. He was very worried, and so was I! To film the two cars with the police officers in them, in the scenes along the Middle Corniche, Hitchcock used a helicopter. That was the first time a helicopter had been used for principal photography. Now it's common but back then it was risky. There were problems resulting from the vibrations; it was necessary to synchronize the shots with the vibrations.

"I have never known another director with such patience. It was remarkable. Hitchcock was always even-tempered. He never got angry. He was really easy-going, pleasant. It effects everything when a director keeps his calm: everything becomes easy. Everyone enjoyed working with Hitchcock....

"With him and Cary Grant, we invented word games: plays on words or funny ways to use them. Hitchcock would think something up, then it would be our turn to make up something different or to create new turns of phrase for him.

"Once or twice I saw the little drawings he made, but that was mostly for the cameraman. Hitchcock always had a definite idea in mind. Occasionally he would change something small to take into account suggestions that were made. Hitchcock was very open. You could discuss or argue about scenes with him, and say, for example, 'That would be easier to film this other way.' But the script was very precise, even for the positioning of actors.[20]

"I often tell this story that points out the differences among directors: When I was making *Mogambo* with John Ford we had been rehearsing a scene where I had to move to a certain spot. Filming began. Then suddenly Ford stopped everything and cried, 'Kelly, what the hell are you doing?' 'Why,' [I answered,] 'I'm going toward the window. It's in the script.' Then Ford yelled at me, '"We're shooting a movie, not a script!"'

Charles Vanel

"I did not know him [Hitchcock] personally. I was contacted by Paramount. I don't know whether he had seen any of my films, but when a director chooses an actor it's because he sees certain qualities in him! He gave me some indications [of what he wanted] before filming began and talked about the character to be played. After filming on the Riviera ended we spent a month in Hollywood shooting in the studio. There were Brigitte Auber [who played Danielle Foussard], Jean Martinelli [her screen father], Georgette Anys [John Robie's housekeeper, Germaine].

"Filming was similar to [what we had experienced] in France. The means of production are much greater,[21] but the work is the same.

"Hitchcock is quite light-hearted by nature, and he has a very pleasant house with the most beautiful collection of French wines you can imagine. He showed them to me and even had me taste some. He really adores that. He and I spoke in French. I don't know if he especially likes to speak French, but since I don't speak English well..."

Brigitte Auber

"Charles Vanel never knew this, but that's not his voice in the film. He had just finished filming *Le Salaire de la peur* [*The Wages of Fear*]. Hitchcock liked his face and hired him thinking he spoke English. Vanel had let on that he spoke it even though he couldn't even say 'yes' and 'no.' Eventually they had to write all his lines in big letters on the sets and you could see his eyes moving [as he read]! That's why Hitch filmed him entirely in closeups.[22] Vanel scarcely opened his mouth, thinking that his lines, which he recited phonetically, would seem more natural that way. Hitch realized that this was not working, and he sent to New York for a French actor who spent two weeks dubbing Vanel, and Vanel never knew!

"Edouard de Segonzac, who was Paramount's representative in France, called me in one day. There was a very large man sitting in an armchair, but I paid no attention to him and chatted with Edouard. The next day I got a call saying that Hitchcock wanted to have lunch with me at the Plaza-Athénée. Hitch and [his wife] Alma were waiting for me at the Plaza and I was surprised when I recognized him. He later told me that the decision to hire me was made during that lunch. When he saw me come in he said, "That's it!" He had seen me in a film by Duvivier, *Sous le ciel de Paris*,[23] where I played a French girl. Since he had noticed the name Madame Sylvie in the titles, he thought that the girl's name was Sylvie and had asked Segonzac to call in all the young actresses with that name. There were three of them, but not the one he wanted.... He did not speak French at all.[24] He only knew how to imitate Maurice Chevalier, rolling his *r*s. Afterward, he learned a bit.

"I love to be directed [but] I had a little squabble with Hitch. We had rehearsed a scene three times, and each time I had played it differently. I asked him which he preferred. He didn't answer. So I just sat down on the floor and said to him: 'If you won't say anything to me, I won't act!' He started to laugh: 'Silly thing, if I have chosen you, it's because you *are* this character. So do as you please.'

"I was jealous of Grace Kelly, because Hitchcock considered her his protégée. He positioned himself on a stool in front of her, indicated how she should speak, manipulated her like a snake charmer. You would have thought of a painter before his canvas....

"Cary Grant helped me by saying 'In the movies, you do as you like.' He made me a list of his first ten films and of the actors whom he imitated. He told me, 'I was so self-conscious, I didn't know what to do with my hands! If I took them out of my pockets it was only to wipe them off nervously, until the day I discovered that in film you must be yourself.' Cary had begun show business in the theater as a dancer and he loved dancing—cha-cha-cha, mambo. The mambo was my favorite, too. Cary brought records to the studio and we danced....

"The scenes between us on the boat were entirely filmed in the studio. There were two rear-projection screens, one on the side and the other above us, with the plane and other shots [seen in the final film]. Now I was wearing a striped sweater that I had picked out with Gladys de Segonzac in a shop on the Rue du Faubourg Saint-Honoré [in Paris]. By chance Cary wore a similar sweater with the same pattern. The scenes with Cary and Grace on the floating platform had been made on location, outdoors; but Hitch had them redone in the studio tank with the water blued and heated because during the location filming, with the sun, the takes were not properly 'matched.'[25] Hitch was sweet to me. He told me, 'You have made great progress in English and, more importantly, you lowered [the timbre of] your voice.' Cary would go over my lines with me. In the scene on the beach at the Hotel Carlton, I was speaking with Cary about Grace. I had to say 'lying on the beach' but I could never pronounce 'beach' as Hitchcock wanted. He cried, 'Accentuate "beach" — "biiiiitch!" Yankees are lazy. Even if you articulate poorly, if you'll accentuate where you need to and keep up the tempo, things will go fine. But if Americans watching the film don't understand, we'll lose them.' Later Hitch explained to me what 'bitch' means.

"The sets for the ball were sumptuous and the roofs were real roofs, slanting down from a height of nearly eighty feet. At the time, I was practicing regularly on the trapeze. I was in top form. For the high angle shot [showing Danielle dangling between the roof and the courtyard below], my hand was attached to Cary's by a leather thong. When my legs were not visible, a platform was slipped under my feet. I spent three days up there. That was very tiring. I explained to Hitch that, in the position where Cary found himself, he would certainly fall forward, and that no one would stay there dangling by one hand without trying to grab on with the other one, but he couldn't care less!

"I don't remember whether it was Hitch or Cary who played this joke on me at the ball. Among the disguised guests I spotted three guys dressed like Dominican friars. I asked if they had been added to the cast. Cary [or Hitch] answered, 'No, they're for you. They'll give you extreme unction if you fall!' I had problems with my thief's black outfits. I had several of them because the tights kept splitting. There was one that had been used by Audrey Hepburn. I was proud to wear that one.

"It was fascinating to see Hitchcock's script. On the left side he sketched each shot with a drawing pencil. That way he could be filming the scene with us on the floating platform and at the same time have an assistant shooting another sequence with two policemen somewhere else. Hitch would say that he didn't need to be there for the film to be made! But all that was the result of great preparation. Hitchcock laughs at logic. At a certain moment, Jean Martinelli is knocked out and thrown into the water. I ask Hitch, 'Who killed my father?' [His answer:] 'What concern is it of yours? I don't know myself, but that adds suspense.'

"The screenplay had been altered and I was not happy. In the first version, Grace was to go back to the States to get divorced. She would bid Cary good-bye and drive off with her mother. John Williams [insurance adjuster Houston] was to say to Cary, 'How charming, that American girl,' with Cary replying, 'A lot of water could flow under the bridge before she comes back!' Then there was an extraordinary scene in prison with Cary and me where I told him that my mother was a thief and that I was born in prison. That was a scene of complicity, an ambiguous scene. With that nostalgic ending you couldn't know for sure whether there was anything going on between the two characters. It was thief to thief. Hitch realized that you couldn't make an audience believe in a couple coming together and then let them drift apart at the end. Although I was furious at the time, now I must admit that it was logical. But the rivalry between the two women would be better explained if that ending had been kept.

"Hitch and I got along famously. My father had recently died. Hitch's daughter had just gotten married. He may have had paternal feelings for me. There was a bond, a rapport. His wife was always there, adorable, like a little mouse.

"Hitch is caustic. He likes to make fun of people. All day long he is in his corner, motionless. And if you sit beside him and listen to him, he will tell you incredible things. He has such a critical eye. In Paris we went to a restaurant together. I asked him whether he was hoping to meet Jacques Becker, [or other] people more interesting than me.[26] Alma laughed and Hitch said, 'They're all the same. I'm no longer into that. I don't need to meet anyone, no matter who.' All day long, he is making jokes, and often dirty jokes for the fun of being scabrous. Cary didn't always find that amusing, nor did I. Cary told me, 'You can't understand; it's American humor.' I didn't care for it; I thought that it degraded Hitch. I think that's his way of shielding himself. Instead of attacking important issues, he stays in his little tower.

"After *To Catch a Thief* I had two more projects with Hitch [which never materialized]. I was supposed to come to Hollywood to make a film about an American soldier in France during the war who brings home a French war bride, but their marriage breaks down. That didn't work out, and Hitch thought of me for the role played by Shirley MacLaine in *The Trouble with Harry*. He told me, 'Since you are typically French, you must make a career for yourself elsewhere, in America or in Italy.'

"During one of his visits to Paris—his American side compels him to always want to be in style—he asked about a 'Buffet.' Since I [thought he meant a piece of furniture and I] knew someone who might sell him a sideboard, I jumped right in and asked Hitch what he wanted. 'Oh, just a big Buffet for my kitchen!' [he replied] 'Something large with his signature.' For a gag, it was a costly one!"[27]

Acknowledgements

These translations appear with permission, as follows: "Hitch, au jour le jour, par Sylvette Baudrot" *Cahiers du Cinéma* no. 39 (October 1954): 14-17, © *Cahiers du Cinéma*; "Petit Journal intime du cinéma (vu de Tourettes-sur-Loup) par André Bazin," *Cahiers du Cinéma* no. 38 (August-September 1954): 36-40, © *Cahiers du Cinéma*; Bruno Villien, *Hitchcock* (Paris: Colona, 1982), selected portions reprinted as *Alfred Hitchcock* (Paris: Rivages, 1985). The author, editor, and publisher gratefully acknowledge the permission granted to reproduce and translate the copyright material in this book. Every effort has been made to trace copyright holders and to obtain permission for the use of copyrighted materials. Please notify the author of any additions or corrections that should be incorporated in any future printing of this material.

For their support of this project I would like to thank Sylvette Baudrot, Bruno Villien, Sidney Gottlieb, Alain Kerzoncuf, Brian Shaffer, Michelle Mattson, Morgane Bordeaux, Stéphanie Carrez, Marylise Caussinus, Shira Malkin, Louisette Palazzolo, Emmanuelle Olivier, Robert Viguier, and Nancy Foltz Vest, as well as staff members at *Cahiers du Cinéma, Le Nouvel Observateur, Opéra*, and Rivages publishers.

Notes

1. For details concerning the difficulties associated with this location shoot, see Steven DeRosa, *Writing with Hitchcock: The Collaboration of Alfred Hitchcock and John Michael Hayes* (New York: Faber and Faber: 2001), 96-124, and James M. Vest, *Hitchcock and France: The Forging of an Auteur* (Westport, CT: Praeger, 2003), 58-79.

2. The phrase "le grand Alfred" appeared in François Truffaut, "Petit Journal intime du cinéma," *Cahiers du Cinéma* no. 37 (July 1954): 34. Hereafter *Cahiers du Cinéma* will be cited as *Cahiers*. On the

French reception of *To Catch a Thief*, pro and con, see Vest, *Hitchcock and France*, 119-26, 131-34.

3. Originally published as "Hitch, au jour le jour," *Cahiers* no. 39 (October 1954): 14-17, translated and printed here in its entirety. Baudrot also authored a book about her career in cinema, *La Script-girl* (Paris: FEMIS, 1989; reprinted 1995). Her annotated shooting scripts for many of the films on which she worked have been collected at the Bibliothèque du Film in Paris. In June 2006, Baudrot returned to the Riviera to visit sites associated with *To Catch a Thief*; her visit was chronicled online, with commentary and photos, by Alain Kerzoncuf and Nàndor Bokor: http://www.hitchcockwiki.com/hitchcock/wiki/Location_trip_to_the_French_Riviera%2C_June_2006.>

4. "Des croquis impératifs," one of which, showing John Robie looking at Danielle on the Hotel Carlton float, was reproduced in *Cahiers*, as an illustration accompanying Baudrot's diary entries ("Hitch, au jour le jour," 14).

5. Unspaced ellipses in the original French texts translated herein, generally indicating a pregnant pause on the part of the speaker, are reproduced in this manner: ...

6. Ultimately, the fireworks and other censurable items remained in the final print; see DeRosa, *Writing with Hitchcock*, 104-05, 116, 122.

7. Saint-Jeannet: a hamlet nestled in the hills north of Vence that served as the locale for Robie's villa; only ten miles from Nice, it is also quite near Tourettes-sur-Loup, where Bazin spent much of the summer of 1954.

8. Saint-Cézaire-sur-Saigne: a hamlet west of Grasse offering panoramic views.

9. Corniche: the steep slopes that rise above the Mediterranean basin along the Riviera, divided into Low, Middle, and High Corniches. Soon after the filming of *To Catch a Thief*, Grace Kelly met Prince Rainier of Monaco, whom she married in 1956; in 1982 an automobile accident on the Corniche claimed her life.

10. See Bazin's account of these events in "Hitchcock contre Hitchcock," *Cahiers* no. 39 (October 1954): 25-32. Bazin's first interview with Hitchcock occurred during filming in the Nice flower market, probably on 18 June. Unsatisfied with Hitchcock's responses, Bazin requested and was granted a second interview a few days later at the Carlton Hotel in Cannes. Bazin acknowledged Baudrot's services as interpreter and ally at both interview sessions (28). Bazin's paraphrase of Hitchcock's remark was slightly different: "How could

he have given me an hour during filming if he had to think about his film at the same time?" (32).

11. As editor of *Cahiers*, Bazin inserted an explanatory footnote at this point in Baudrot's account (bottom of p. 16).

Here is how that second interview ended. Hitchcock said "Au revoir, Monsieur" in French, but pronounced "Monsieur" in a strange way, giving the impression of something like "Meniour," articulated with pursed lips and with affectation. He repeated this several times while glancing at Sylvette Baudrot, who, it seemed to me, didn't understand much better than I. Then, laughing, Hitchcock explained to her that he enjoyed saying to his French interlocutors, no matter what the subject, "Bonjour, Meniour," "Oui, Meniour," "Merci beaucoup, Meniour," as if he did not know how to pronounce "Monsieur." Actually, since the French word *fumier* is *manure* in English, he was able to treat every Frenchman as *fumier* while maintaining a polite air. That little private joke conveys rather precisely the tone of pleasantries typical of A. Hitchcock, which help pass the time with his collaborators between shots. Naturally I'll leave the door open for other interpretations, favorable to my opponents. Indeed that parting shot could retroactively throw a veil of ironic scorn on the role that I had been playing [during our interviews].

Later in this same issue of *Cahiers*, Bazin explained that he had tried during these two interviews to "accost" Hitchcock with the radical idea—espoused by François Truffaut, Eric Rohmer, Claude Chabrol, and other staff writers at *Cahiers*—that Hitchcock's films exhibited a uniquely personal artistic style and a persistent vision involving an exchange of guilt between a weaker character and a stronger one, a view that Bazin himself found unconvincing (see "Hitchcock contre Hitchcock," 27-30).

12. Baudrot's French transcription, translated here, corresponds to the English version of a cable dated 8 July 1954, partially reproduced in DeRosa, *Writing with Hitchcock*, 115-16; the last three sentences cited here do not appear in DeRosa's version.

13. Selections from "Petit Journal intime du cinéma (vu de Tourettes-sur-Loup)," *Cahiers* no. 38 (August-September 1954): 36-40. Only those portions concerning *To Catch a Thief* are reproduced

here. Omissions of unrelated materials are indicated with three spaced periods, as follows: . . .

14. Jacques Doniol-Valcroze was, with Bazin, a founding editor of *Cahiers*. Tourettes, whose name justly conjures visions of medieval parapets overlooking the gorges of the Wolf River, is located north of Cannes, nestled among terraces covered with violets in the perfume-producing region between Saint-Paul and Grasse.

15. Founded during the Occupation by activists in the French Resistance, *L'Ecran Français* was an influential weekly that championed the Ciné-Club movement and encouraged would-be filmmakers. In 1948 it published Alexandre Astruc's seminal article proposing the concept of the "caméra-stylo." Its coverage of Hitchcock films included stinging critiques by Bazin—e.g., of *Shadow of a Doubt* (no. 14 [3 October 1945]: 6) and *Suspicion* (no. 70 [29 October 1946]: 6)—as well as Bazin's scathing summary "Panoramique sur Hitchcock" (no. 238 [23 January 1950]: 8-9). Like Bazin, Timmory and Chazal were outspoken critics of Hitchcock's work. Timmory's review of *Rope* labeled Hitchcock a swindler and castigated him for lack of originality ("Hitchcock, le vénéneux," no. 243 [27 February 1950]: 11). In his review of *To Catch a Thief*, Chazal opined that the stunning Riviera scenery and the fine acting of French performers compensated for the flaccid, suspenseless screenplay (*Paris-Presse* [27 December 1955]: 5). The weekly *Cinémonde* began in 1928, suspended publication from 1940 until 1946, then continued until 1970.

16. Gréolières: a picturesque Hamlet upriver from Tourettes. Cagnes-sur-mer: port city west of Nice, where a local cleric, Honoré Gaglio, presided over the interment scenes in *To Catch a Thief*. The luxurious Carlton Hotel at Cannes was featured in several scenes in the film.

17. Bazin's musings reflected impressions and suppositions, some inaccurate, recorded during filming by an observant critic without access to a shooting script.

18. The convoluted sentence reads: "Pis encore, en son absence, il ne s'agit pas de ne pas faire exactement ce qui était prévu."

19. Interviews with Grace Kelly, Charles Vanel, and Brigitte Auber from Bruno Villien, *Hitchcock* (Paris: Colona, 1982), 252-59, translated and presented in their entirety.

20. "Même pour les positions": In French interviews, Hitchcock's own use of the term "position" suggests that in his mind it includes not only blocking of actors and props, but also

camera angle and framing; see, for example, his comments on "la position" and his illustrative drawings in François Truffaut and Claude Chabrol, "Entretien avec Alfred Hitchcock," *Cahiers* no. 44 (February 1955): 24-25.

21. "On tourne avec beaucoup plus de moyens," presumably referring to the advanced technical support, bigger staffs, and larger budgets of Hollywood filmmaking.

22. This problem was addressed in various ways in different shots; in several instances the camera angle allowed Vanel's mouth to be partially or totally obscured as he spoke. Eventually his lines were overdubbed by Jean Duval (see DeRosa, *Writing with Hitchcock*, 116-17).

23. Julien Duvivier (1896-1967): celebrated French director of the 1930s who came to Hollywood during World War II; his films include *Poil de Carotte* (1925 and 1932), *Pépé le Moko* (1937), and *Sous le ciel de Paris* [*Under the Paris Sky*] (1951).

24. Compare the contradictory information supplied by Vanel, above; other sources—including correspondence with Truffaut and recordings of his renditions of favorite anecdotes in French—indicate that Hitchcock's written and spoken French were quite passable. Yet he could play "dumb" when he wished.

25. "Pas 'raccord,' " (a shortened form of "raccordé[e]s," commonly used in filmmaking), i.e., improperly aligned or out of sync.

26. Jacques Becker (1906-1960): French filmmaker, assistant to Jean Renoir in the 1930s, known for sophisticated comedies; his films include *Goupi Mains Rouges* (1942), *Casque d'Or* (1951), and *The Adventures of Arsène Lupin* (1956).

27. This multi-layered joke centers on divergent meanings of "buffet/Buffet," which in oral speech could be understood to refer either to a large hutch or to a painter of that name, or to that artist's work. At first Auber thought Hitchcock was talking about furniture, whereas he actually meant a painting. In the end she turned the joke back on its author; the painting would be costly, and so would his jesting: "Pour un gag, c'était cher payé!" The reference is probably to Bernard Buffet (1928-99), known for his oversized canvases, strong dark lines, angular figures, and enormous signature; but it might refer to Jean Dubuffet (1901-85), a painter who developed a theory of "l'art brut" that incorporated non-traditional materials such as asphalt, coal, and sand. In French the latter is generally referred to as Dubuffet and the former as Buffet, but this distinction is not always respected by English speakers. Donald Spoto reports that

Hitchcock commissioned a Dubuffet that was never executed (*The Dark Side of Genius* [New York: Da Capo, 1999], 493); Connie Bruck mentions a Bernard Buffet portrait of agent-associate Lew Wasserman, commissioned by Hitchcock, that hung in the Wassermans' foyer (*When Hollywood had a King* [New York: Random House, 2003], 162-63); Bill Krohn's inventory of Hitchcock's art collection ("Le Musée secret de monsieur Hitchcock," *Cahiers* no. 559 [July-August 2001]: 67-74) lists an oil painting by Bernard Buffet, *Fleurs dans un vase sur une table*, but no Dubuffet.

JAMES MACDOWELL

What We Don't See, and What We Think it Means: Ellipsis and Occlusion in Rear Window

JEFF: Anybody actually see the wife get on the train?
DOYLE: I hate to remind you, but this all got started because you said she was murdered. Now did anyone, including you, actually see her murdered?

Rear Window (1954) contains a total of eighteen ellipses between its scenes, all of them conveyed by a fade-out/fade-in, even at moments when a dissolve might seem a more conventional choice.[1] It is unusual for a sound film to exclusively use the black screen to denote elapsed time, not least in the contemporaneous work of Hitchcock: of the twelve films he made between 1950 and 1960, for example, no other employs only the fade-out/fade-in to communicate ellipses. I can suggest at least three possible reasons for this atypical stylistic choice, each concerning a separate issue on which ellipses can have a bearing. The first relates to broader conventions of ellipsis and is a matter of the film's clarity of storytelling. A dissolve and a fade-out/fade-in are the two most commonly used transitions in the "classical" Hollywood cinema for conveying a passage of unseen time (a cut tending to establish immediate succession). Of these, the latter's visual gap conveys for the spectator a more emphatic distinction between action just witnessed and action to follow than does the former's visual link; it therefore makes sense for a film with no possibility of disambiguating one scene from another via location (because set almost entirely in one room) to use this device to help its spectators orient themselves temporally.

The second reason relates to issues of mood and point of view, and to the fact that, as Donald Spoto has said, *Rear Window*'s "constant fades to black contribute to the dreamlike, tenebrous quality of the whole film."[2] To Spoto's observation, I would merely add that the rather "dreamlike" nature of the fade-out/fade-ins also acts as one more strategy that helps align our experience with that of a protagonist whom we see sleeping and awaking unusually often. Finally, it seems thematically fitting that a film which places so much importance on the unseen should periodically impose an almost literal blindness on its audience (particularly its original cinema audience). The choice seems especially apt, given that it is during these moments of darkness that many of the story's most crucial events take place and go unseen by almost all its characters.

Since Hitchcock was, as Eric Rohmer and Claude Chabrol have said, "one of the greatest inventors of forms in the entire history of cinema," it should come as no surprise that he was aware of the diverse functions ellipses can be made to serve in narrative film.[3] In this essay I hope to show that we can at the very least confidently say that the understanding of this technical device he displays in his work certainly outstrips that of film scholarship to date. The ellipsis has seldom been openly addressed by film studies, and when it has, it has tended to be treated in a manner that over-emphasizes its negative or purely instrumental qualities, as I will discuss. By contrast, I will be arguing that Hitchcock's cinema should encourage us to see ellipses and other forms of elision as having the potential to be key *expressive* features in a filmmaker's arsenal. I suggested above that we should ask why particular types of transition are used in a particular film: this is an example of just one issue relating to ellipsis that has seldom been considered in detail, and I will dedicate myself here to raising a number of others. Through an analysis of ellipsis and other elisions in *Rear Window*, I will begin a discussion about what Hitchcock's uses of these rhetorical features can teach us as film scholars—both about some under-acknowledged aspects of this often-discussed film, and about ellipses more generally. First, though, a few words about my approach.

Ellipsis in Film Studies

In *The Classical Hollywood Cinema*, David Bordwell offers the following description of how ellipses tend to function:

> In the sound era, fades and dissolves were the most common signs of temporal ellipsis . . . Such optical punctuation marks can be compared with theatrical or literary conventions (curtain, end of chapter). . . Punctuation marks enable the narration to skip unimportant intervals by simple omission.[4]

It is, clearly, one common practice for a portion of time to be elided so that we may move from one scene to the next without having to experience the "unimportant" events that occurred in the interim. This is, as Bordwell says, "normal operating procedure."[5] Hitchcock himself famously called drama "life with the dull bits cut out," and *Rear Window* certainly uses such "normal" temporal ellipses to pass over "unimportant" events.[6] This film also, however, elides action in more ways, and for more complex reasons, than can be accounted for by this formulation. Not only this, but *Rear Window* also shows us that "normal" temporal ellipses can themselves assume a great deal more significance than *The Classical Hollywood Cinema*'s schema would allow. In *Narration in the Fiction Film*, Bordwell discusses ellipses at greater length, and delineates a number of possible functions they can be made to serve. However, all the (certainly both accurate and valuable) models he proposes are still concerned purely with accounting for the different ways a film's plot (in Bordwell's terms, its *syuzhet*) can either condense or elongate the time it takes to tell the story (*fabula*) it depicts.[7] In part because of this work already done by Bordwell, my own approach is able to move beyond matters of temporal condensation and elongation and toward a focus on other expressive possibilities of ellipsis that he does not address. In particular, I am interested in examining the roles different devices can be made to play in the communication and creation of *Rear Window*'s point of view, narrative focus, and themes.

Two beliefs underwrite my own understanding of ellipsis: first, that fiction films create a fictional world; second, that a film's point of view determines our access to and relationship with that world. An appreciation of film worlds can help us to explain why what goes unseen in a film will routinely form as large a part of our understanding of its story as what is seen. This is because it rightly places an emphasis on the continuation of an imagined world beyond the limits of what we actually see represented. In his recent work on film worlds, V.F. Perkins notes that

> We are offered an assembly of bits and pieces from which to compose a world. Fragmentary representation yields an imagined solidity and extensiveness. The malleability of the image is in a reciprocal relationship with the seamlessness and continuity that the image can evoke in our minds. Our imagination of the world is impressively independent of the means of representation.[8]

In the same way as we always unavoidably imagine and take into account the off-screen world that we presume exists beyond a particular shot or sequence, so do we automatically presuppose the continuation of this world *in between* the pieces of "fragmentary representation" we are shown. Given this, we should not (and *cannot*) exclude implied, but unseen, aspects of a world from our understanding of a film's whole. As such, my following discussion will often make references to *Rear Window*'s world in order to discuss aspects of its story that go unrepresented.

Yet the fact still remains that those aspects of a world contained within ellipses, or elided in any other way, *are* indeed unrepresented. It is here that an awareness of point of view becomes useful. The meaning I intend for point of view is essentially that offered by George M. Wilson in *Narration in Light*: "the different ways in which a form of narration can systematically structure an audience's overall epistemic access to narrative."[9] An ellipsis or elision is first and foremost a considered element of a film's narration that withholds story information. What is withheld can be important to the establishment of a film's point of view in several ways. First, using the terms laid out by Douglas Pye in his work on the subject, we can say that an ellipsis will always affect the "temporal axis" of point of view. This axis, which dictates our understanding of how time behaves in a film, is where an ellipsis' most basic function will be felt: it will, as Pye says, "signify gaps in time . . . so that the spectator's and the characters' times diverge." However, an ellipsis will also necessarily affect what Pye has termed a film's "cognitive axis," which has ramifications for our overall epistemic relationship with the film.[10] That is to say, what is withheld will have a direct impact on, for example, our sense of which events and which people the film deems important, and on whether we are permitted to know more or less than particular characters at particular times. This axis is clearly particularly useful for any discussion of Hitchcock's work, since it can be so key in creating suspense, and especially central in the case of *Rear Window*, given that the film's point of view ensures we share an unusually (though not unqualifiedly) close epistemic experience with its protagonist.

So far I have been discussing just one method of elision: temporal ellipsis. However, it is certainly not only through denying a portion of time that a film can elide that which it does not want us to see: a similar effect can also be achieved through denying a particular view of its world.

Hitchcock and Constrained Viewpoints

In one sense, every shot of every film constitutes a constrained viewpoint, since the presentation of one view necessarily means the denial of all others. Yet very different kinds of emphasis can be created through different kinds of constrained viewpoint. We come close to grasping the available poles if we imagine the difference between an event that goes unseen because it takes place a hundred miles away from where the camera is pointed, and an event that is elided by a hand covering the camera's lens: the former denies a potential viewpoint spatially, while the latter denies a view through an overt obstruction. Hitchcock's films, which so often strive to create suspense and menace via implication, must routinely find techniques of strategically withholding information that exist somewhere between these poles. Think, for example, of the cut away in *Secret Agent* (1936) to Ashenden (John Gielgud) in the observatory at the moment of the mountaintop murder, or of the extreme long-shot that conceals the identity of who it is that falls from Westminster Cathedral in *Foreign Correspondent* (1940), or the retreating camera that denies us the sight of Rusk (Barry Foster) killing Barbara (Anna Massey) in *Frenzy* (1972). In the sense that each withholds information from us visually, we might refer to all these moments as examples of differing strategies of visual elision. Since my discussion will require me to repeatedly draw upon one method of such elision in particular, it is worth briefly placing it in the context of some other constrained viewpoints used by Hitchcock.

The extent to which certain kinds of constrained viewpoint will seem to be elisions at all may depend on context. For instance, when Scottie (James Stewart) first sees Madeleine (Kim Novak) apparently fall to her death in *Vertigo* (1958), we will not, until our second viewing, realize that a vital event is being elided through the film's refusal to show us what takes place in the bell tower. Only later, after we learn what occurred only a few feet away, might we recognize that the film misdirected us through its point of view being closely tied to Scottie. While it is entirely possible for this kind of restricted viewpoint to go unnoticed, other kinds of visual elision may be more obvious, such as the camera movement in *Psycho* (1960) that cranes up to a bird's eye view of Norman (Anthony Perkins) carrying Mother down the stairs. Again, we do not on first viewing realize that the angle is used to deny us a clear view of Mother, but we do nonetheless notice the device that restricts our viewpoint—if not yet its significance. A visual *obstruction*, meanwhile, is far more likely to be recognized as such. In *Blackmail* (1929), for example, we are denied a view of the attempted rape of Alice (Anny Ondra) and the murder of her attacker (Cyril Ritchard) because both take place behind a curtain that lets us see only the frantic ripples caused by the violence behind it, Alice's hand emerging to grab a knife, and eventually the attacker's arm slumping down, limp and lifeless.

This last strategy of elision is very much presented *as* an elision, and in this sense is more comparable to a traditional ellipsis than those of either *Vertigo* or *Psycho*. This device is one that I wish to draw on during my discussion as a helpful tool for analysis, and I will be referring to it as an "occlusion." I take this term to mean an instance in which our view of something is denied, despite the camera being pointed directly at it, due to some form of obstruction. I hope to demonstrate through my discussion of *Rear Window* both that an occlusion can serve storytelling functions similar enough to warrant comparison to an ellipsis, and that it is a concept that can help increase our understanding of the unseen in film. In order to help me in this, I shall now expand on some of the many purposes Hitchcock is able to make occlusions and ellipses serve by looking at a series of short scenes that employ both devices rather extensively.

Storytelling and Point of View

The portion of *Rear Window* that contains the most ellipses in the shortest space of time takes place following the meal delivered to Jeff and Lisa from the Twenty-One club. Jeff has told Lisa his doubts about their relationship, and, despite his request that they "keep things status quo," Lisa has left. Sitting alone, Jeff turns to his window, then hears a scream and a crash come from somewhere outside, before proceeding to drift in and out of sleep for the majority of the night. In many ways the short scenes that follow are the most important for the film's story thus far, since they together mark the point at which Jeff begins to be concerned with the goings-on outside his window, and thus begin the investigation that will eventually lead not only to the solving of the murder but also to the ultimate romantic reunion of Lisa and Jeff.

The first fade-out fulfills the "italics" function that an ellipsis can serve, pointedly emphasizing the importance of the scream.[11] It is made to do this by following a cut from a shot of the courtyard (in which the camera changes direction and pace suddenly when the scream is heard) to a medium shot of Jeff scanning the scene worriedly. Were the ellipsis to come slightly later, after Jeff stopped pondering what he heard (as he must have done, since the next time we see him he is asleep), the scream would carry far less dramatic weight. This is thus the first time an ellipsis has been linked with what we will later discover has been an act of violence—something that will happen repeatedly in different ways throughout the film. When we fade in again, we are positioned slightly further away from a now-sleeping Jeff. These two sequential shots, and the split-second of black between them, convey that an unspecified amount time has passed—time in which, unbeknownst to us, something has taken place that will alter a great deal in the film's world. As will become clear, the events that occur during this ellipsis are far from "unimportant"; in fact, they are the central catalyst for change in the story, and will reverberate until the end of the film.

This large, unseen change is then partially echoed in other smaller, visible changes that have occurred or are about to occur. While the scream potentially hinted at a change in the film's mood—away from the relatively light romantic drama that we have so far seen, toward a darker, more typically Hitchcockian thriller—so has there been a change in the world's atmosphere: we hear the rumble of thunder in the air, and rain begins to fall. This change that has been taking place during the ellipsis then forces another change to a routine, when the couple whom we have previously seen sleeping on their fire escape are forced inside by the weather. Similarly, when, a few moments later, Thorwald (at this point known only as "the salesman") leaves his apartment with a suitcase, it is his deviation from a norm that attracts Jeff's heightened attention. It is fitting that the term "status quo" should have been spoken barely two minutes before we witness all these small changes in routine. Since we later learn that Thorwald was likely dismembering his wife in the period between the previous scene and this one, a very great change indeed in the film's equilibrium has gone unseen during this ellipsis.

Yet, crucially, it is not the omission of a span of time alone that allows this event to go unseen. The constraints that the film's point of view has established so far (our confinement to Jeff's apartment and the view from it) mean that, even were we to have witnessed every passing second of the elided period, we would still not have seen what Thorwald did in his apartment, assuming his shades were drawn. The apparent significance of the temporal elision is therefore lessened by the spectator's acceptance of the terms of visual restriction the film has already established. This skillfully ensures that we do not regard the omitted time span as a conspicuous absence, and chimes with one of Hitchcock's expressed views on storytelling: "I'm a great believer in making sure that, if people see the film a second time, they don't feel cheated. . . . You must be honest about it and not merely keep things away from an audience."[12] Clearly, this approach (and other of Hitchcock's elisions) does in fact "keep things away" from the audience, but does so in such a subtle and logically justifiable way that no viewer could ever rightly feel "cheated" by the refusal of information, were he or she to re-watch the film.

Similarly, at the end of the scene a palpable question hangs in the air—Where is Thorwald going?—which we fully expect to go unanswered due to the constrained viewpoint that we have come to expect. It is clear from the intrigued look on his face and the attentiveness of his gaze that Jeff too is concerned with this question. He lifts his wrist and looks down at his watch. The film then fades out on a close-up of his wristwatch showing the time as 1:55, before fading in on virtually the same shot, but with the watch now showing 2:35. From this shot there is a cut to Jeff looking up from his watch, then to a view of Thorwald, who has by this point arrived back at the corridor on his floor of the apartment block. This ellipsis therefore not only conveys that forty minutes have passed, but also confers greater significance on those forty minutes by letting us know that Jeff has been timing them. The ellipsis is thus made to serve a number of important storytelling functions: (1) it communicates Jeff's growing interest in what is going on outside his window; (2) it similarly begins *our* speculations about the unseen that will characterize much of the film's hold over us; and (3) it is the first point at which we have been encouraged to associate the unseen specifically with Thorwald.

Yet, once again, we are not at this moment encouraged to speculate about what we might have been permitted to see during these forty elapsed minutes—the interior of, and view from, Jeff's apartment—but rather about what has happened in another, unknown location. This means that Thorwald's movements are not even truly elided by the film in the "normal" sense, since it would likely have been impossible to see them even if we had been witness to the missing forty minutes of the film's world. Therefore, despite the foregrounding of elapsed time, the epistemic frustration here is not in fact caused by a durational gap, but rather a visual and spatial one. This distinction is important for establishing the audience's relationship to the workings of occlusion, which the film will come to repeatedly exploit.

When Thorwald reenters his apartment, the closed blinds of his window conceal his movements, causing a brief instance of occlusion (fig. 1). Because of the film's structures of point of view, we know that this occlusion would almost certainly continue were the camera to remain focused on Thorwald's window. Instead, however, Jeff's—and our—view moves momentarily to the composer and his drunken antics, before returning to Thorwald in time to see him leave again. We then cut back to Jeff, a speculative look on his face, and

Figure 1

fade-out. The brief occlusion here acts in a different way from the one from *Blackmail* I cited earlier. In *Blackmail*, there are two main reasons why our view must remain on the obscuring curtain: to build suspense about the outcome of a struggle we know is going on behind it, and because the film has established no conventions of point of view that would allow Hitchcock to cut to anything else without seriously confusing or frustrating his audience. At this moment in *Rear Window*, by contrast, Hitchcock cuts away from the occlusion to the composer in order to (1) not bore his audience by making them look at a covered window for thirty seconds, (2) not yet encourage excessively serious speculation about Thorwald's actions (all we currently know is that he is going out late with a suitcase), and, most importantly, (3) reinforce again the fact that our view of the opposite apartments is to a great extent dependent on what Jeff can and cannot see. It is unlikely that Jeff himself would at this early stage stay glued to the occlusion provided by the blinds, and as a consequence (our interest having been frustrated as well as his) neither do we. Just as we would have been unable to see where Thorwald went even without the earlier ellipsis between the shots of the watch, so would we be denied a view of his actions in the apartment even if we were to remain looking directly at his window. In this way, both that ellipsis and this occlusion act to strengthen our cognitive and epistemic alignment with Jeff.

After the fade-in at the beginning of the following scene, we see Jeff with his eyes closed, asleep, before he abruptly awakens. This creates the sense that the time during which he was asleep was unimportant to the story: it is only now that he is waking that we need rejoin the film's world. He immediately looks out towards Thorwald's window, as if afraid that he may have missed something in the interim; if the film has succeeded in intriguing us with Thorwald's late-night trip, we are likely to wonder the same thing. There is then a cut to a shot showing the window, the blinds still down. We do not know at this point whether Thorwald is in his apartment and we have missed his return, or whether he has yet to come back. If it is the former, then the temporal elision we have just undergone served to conceal this information; if the latter, then we would not have seen Thorwald regardless of the ellipsis, and we have merely skipped an "unimportant interval." The latter turns out to be the case, since after we have seen Miss Torso return home and dispense with an over-amorous admirer, Thorwald makes his reentrance and disappears behind the blinds again, hidden from view. Jeff now falls asleep. There is then a cut to a shot that pans to show us Thorwald's covered apartment window; fade-out. We thus, for a moment, see here something that Jeff cannot, telling us both that we are still largely confined by the viewpoint we have come to expect (the occlusion caused by a closed blind still applies), but that our visual access to what goes on outside the window is now not dependent purely on Jeff, but on the film's own design.

The next scene continues to privilege our view over Jeff's. We fade-in on a shot that reveals him asleep, before panning over to the window to let us see Thorwald leaving his apartment with a woman. This unavoidably feels like an important revelation of information, since it grants us a partial view of what will later come to be a frustrating ellipsis for Jeff himself.[13] Yet, on second viewing, we can see that it also acts to distract us from something concealed by the preceding ellipsis: this woman *entering* the apartment. This moment therefore misleads us by giving us a relatively privileged view, while also acting as a sleight-of-hand that uses our understanding of the film's conventions of point of view against us. This is in fact a variation on a technique Hitchcock often used in various ways throughout his career. Speaking of *North By Northwest* (1959), Susan Smith says:

> The film's strategy of surprising us with information withheld from the male protagonist has the effect of misleading even as it appears to privilege, for it lulls us into believing that we have been given a much superior epistemic position than is actually the case. The advance release of key information disguises the extent to which this information is still only partial by creating an impression in our mind of having been privileged with all that it is necessary to know.[14]

In the case of the moment in *Rear Window*, it is to a large extent our knowledge of the film's established conventions of ellipsis that allows Hitchcock to achieve this characteristic misdirection. Until now the fact that the film's point of view has restricted our view of Thorwald to that which Jeff also sees has meant that we have been the denied any moments when Jeff *cannot* see him, via either an ellipsis or occlusion. Therefore, the fact that we are now privy to an event that we might reasonably expect to have been elided encourages us to feel an unjustified degree of cognitive superiority to Jeff. It is thus the overt rejection of one possible ellipsis here that discourages us from speculating about another, "covert," ellipsis that we have unknowingly undergone.

Ellipses, then, are certainly not being used in this series of short scenes merely to "skip unimportant intervals," but rather as complex storytelling devices with many possible rhetorical uses. It is perhaps unsurprising that *Rear Window* should provide fertile ground for ellipses since it is, famously, a film in which speculation about the unseen plays a key narrative and thematic role—as the scenes I have discussed make abundantly clear. Indeed, I decided to begin my analysis with this sequence precisely because it does so clearly use ellipses (and occlusions) to achieve more functions than are accounted for by *The Classical Hollywood Cinema*'s definition. I now wish to look, however, at some ways in which Hitchcock is also able to make "normal" temporal ellipses (those which do apparently simply "skip unimportant intervals") convey more than merely elapsed time. To illustrate my point, let us briefly look at an ellipsis that occurs before speculation about the unseen has assumed such major significance to the film's story.

"Normal" Temporal Ellipsis and Narrative Focus

The ellipsis between the shot of Stella reprimanding Jeff for spying on the newlyweds' romantic rituals ("Window shopper!") and a panning shot of the courtyard (which eventually leads us back through the window for a view of the sleeping Jeff) is conveyed by a fade-out, then a subsequent fade-in barely a second later. Within this split-second of black screen, several hours have passed in the story's world. Whereas the first scene took place in the morning, it is now dusk: the sky is a dark orange, the inhabitants of the courtyard are turning on their lights, and a lit street lamp is visible through the gap between the buildings.

What has happened in *Rear Window*'s world during this ellipsis? As far as we can know for certain, very little other than a change from morning to evening. From a glimpse into Miss Torso's window, we see that she has changed from the white underwear or bathing suit she was previously wearing into some black evening-wear; the medium shot of Jeff with Lisa's shadow creeping up him shows that he has also changed his clothes (his shirt is now grey, rather than the earlier blue); and as the scene develops we can also assume that Stella must have left his apartment, and Lisa must have entered. This is the sum total of the events that we can initially be sure of, based on the information given. As far as we know, Jeff himself has done nothing during the entire day except change his shirt, turn his chair around, and fall asleep.

However, although nothing of any apparent significance has occurred during this ellipsis, it is in fact very important that we are not encouraged to speculate about anything else that Jeff might have done during this "unimportant" elided time. This sense that Jeff is seemingly doing nothing between scenes in fact recurs consistently throughout the film. While other characters come into and leave the apartment, living their ongoing lives during the various ellipses, we assume that Jeff is almost entirely inactive when not on screen. He does not work (as Lisa does), investigate leads (as Lisa and Doyle do), go home to a spouse (as Stella presumably does, to Miles), and—especially—not murder anyone (as Thorwald does). As we saw in the series of scenes just under discussion, the question was always what Thorwald had been doing in the elapsed time, not what Jeff may or may not have done. The ellipsis book-ended by the shots of the watch probably illustrates this most clearly: we see Jeff look down at his wristwatch when Thorwald leaves, then forty minutes later see him look up from it when Thorwald returns (figs. 2 and 3). It appears almost as if he has been in suspended animation throughout all the elided minutes. That we are never encouraged to imagine any actions that he may have carried out in between scenes serves partly to establish and reestablish the fact of his dull incapacitation (and that he consequently has, as he tells Gunnison, "nothing to do but look out the window at the neighbors"), thus increasing the plausibility—and slightly lessening the perversity—of his continual spying. It also, however, firmly consolidates his position as our protagonist and our close relationship with him. Many critics have suggested that we are made to identify with Jeff by the association of our viewpoint with his as regards what is seen from his window. What seems equally important to me is, first, that he is present in every single scene of the film and, second, that we are seemingly by his side for each and every noteworthy thing he does during the narrative's time-frame (with the possible exception of a final trip to hospital that provides him with his second cast). By suggesting that he does nothing of importance other than that

Figure 2

Figure 3

which we too share in, the ellipses in the film act to draw us closer to a Jeff-centric view of *Rear Window*'s world.

The sense that Jeff has been inactive during the time implied by the "window shopper" ellipsis is heightened via the contrast with Lisa and what we soon learn of her accomplishments during the elapsed time. After her plan to surprise him with a dinner from Twenty One has come off smoothly, Lisa lets us know she has been doing a great deal since the morning:

> What a day I've had! . . . I was all morning in a sales
> meeting, and then I had to dash to the Waldorf for a

quick drink with Madame Dufresne . . . then I had to go to lunch with the *Harpers Bazaar* people, and that's when I ordered dinner; and then I had two fall showings twenty blocks apart; then I had to have a cocktail with Leland and Slim Hayward . . . and then I had to dash back and change.

The manner in which this information is relayed, with the constant repetition of "and then" before each new event, stresses the continual passing of time (as well as the sheer number of things she has accomplished), but it also rushes through this time and condenses it to a mere list. We therefore recognize that her time during the ellipsis has been filled to the brim, while also immediately sensing that what she has been doing is relatively unimportant for our understanding of the story. The pace and lack of elaborating detail mean that we focus very little on what she is actually recounting, and are certainly not encouraged to try to imagine the places or people she has seen. Jeff in fact draws attention to the film's own sidelining of such matters when he mockingly asks for further information: "Now tell me, *tell* me: what was Mrs. Dufresne *wearing?*" He does not really want to know the answer to this question, and neither, as it were, does the film; as a result, Lisa is cut off in the middle of answering ("Oh, she was wearing the most marvelous Italian silk—"; "Oh, *Italian?*"). Whether this lack of interest in Lisa's work is intended to translate (perhaps in an instance of somewhat sexist presumption) to the audience, or whether we are invited to regard it critically is a question of point of view that each viewer must answer for him or herself.[15] Either way, we can certainly say that Lisa's brief description of what she has been up to during the ellipsis widens our conception of *Rear Window*'s world, but does so in a way that stresses that it is Jeff's, not her, experience of this world that will largely be our focus. Hitchcock (and screenwriter John Michael Hayes) thus here demonstrates that the manner in which a film allows us to subsequently learn of an ellipsis's content is one more way in which it can (in this case, retrospectively) assume significance.

Thematic Functions

I have already demonstrated that Jeff's apparent inactivity during ellipses serves as one means of communicating that he is to command the film's main focus. However, another reward of his transparency—the fact we are apparently witness to virtually everything of note that he does during the narrative— is something akin to *trustworthiness*. Unlike Thorwald, Jeff never seems at all mysterious, or in any sense untrustworthy, because of what we cannot see of him. Since he seemingly takes no significant actions whatsoever during time when he is not visible to us, we are given no reason or opportunity to doubt him. By contrast, Thorwald's trustworthiness is in constant doubt, and this is caused in large part by the fact that we are allowed to speculate that he may be doing a great deal during the times when we cannot see him. Arthur Laurents, the screenwriter of *Rope* (1948), said of Hitchcock that "he thought everyone was doing something physical and nasty behind every closed door," and *Rear Window* seems absolutely to bear out this paranoia about the unseen.[16] Virtually all of the violent or sinister events that occur in the film do so either during ellipses, during occlusions, or in ways that stress the impermissibility of viewing them clearly. The very first suggestion of danger and suspense in the film, the ominous shadow across Jeff at the opening of the scene discussed above, is made possible only by the ellipsis which covers Lisa's entrance into the apartment. More obviously, of course, the dismemberment (and perhaps the actual murder) of Anna Thorwald also happens in an ellipsis. Equally, the second killing, that of the dog, occurs during an ellipsis too, and while Jeff's blinds are down: we fade out on a shot of Lisa going into the bedroom to change, then fade in for her slinky reentrance, only for the couple's flirting to be interrupted by the piercing scream of the dog's owner.

There are also occlusions that convey this sense of the unseen being a dangerous thing. As I have demonstrated, at least one occlusion (caused by Thorwald's blinds) presumably conceals the act of body parts being loaded into a suitcase.

Figure 4

Two of the tensest moments during Lisa's break-in to Thorwald's apartment are also caused by occlusions. First, the portion of wall that separates the living room from his bedroom is used to obscure Lisa's hiding place so that we are unsure of where she is and of how likely Thorwald is to discover her as he moves through to his room. The few seconds during which Thorwald briefly passes behind the wall and emerges on the other side to discover the handbag laid on the bed, still apparently unaware of Lisa's presence, are among the most suspenseful of the film (fig. 4). This moment is then closely followed by another that uses the tenets of occlusion to create a sickening anxiety: Thorwald turning off the lights when Lisa screams so he can continue beating her in darkness. This is not quite a full occlusion, in that we can still make out some of Lisa and Thorwald as they struggle, but the principles it uses are the same.

Not occlusions, but still pointed visual restrictions, are also partially responsible for Lisa finding herself in this predicament in the first place. While our view is restricted to Lisa searching Thorwald's apartment (and Stella and Jeff watching this), Miss Lonelyhearts makes her final preparations for suicide, meaning Stella and Jeff miss it until it is almost too late. Moments later, another instance of misdirection (the characters, and we, being focused on the apartments of Miss Lonelyhearts and the composer at the time) mean that they, and we, also miss Thorwald returning to the apartment block until he is right outside his door. It is worth remembering too that the two violent incidents in the film that we *do* see also take place in ways that draw attention to the difficulty we have in seeing them clearly: the near-rape of Miss Lonelyhearts (partly obscured by window blinds), and Thorwald's attack on Jeff in the penultimate scene (in darkness, and periodically blotted-out by light-bulb flashes). In this way, the film repeatedly equates the unseen with the dangerous, violent aspects of its world—what Robin Wood has termed Hitchcock's "chaos world"—by suggesting that it is during elisions that these aspects are likely to be realized most threateningly.[17]

Besides violence, the other theme in *Rear Window* that is linked with the unseen via ellipses and occlusions is sex. The first instance of this is an occlusion, and occurs during the film's second scene, when Jeff sees two attractive young women preparing to sunbathe naked on the roof of the opposite apartment block, an act presented in such a way that we (and Jeff) see only removed items of clothing being hung over a railing (fig. 5). The newlyweds are important in this regard too, since their suggested perpetual routine of sex is alluded to several times via the occlusion of their closed window blind. Their unseen sexual activity is also unwittingly linked by Lisa to notions of danger when she says, "For all you know there's probably something a lot more sinister going on behind *those* windows." The interchangeable nature of sex and violence when one cannot see, but only imagine, either is again specifically vocalized in a conversation in which Jeff suggests that Thorwald's peculiar movements point to an unseen murder, while Lisa repeatedly implies that they point to unseen sex: "Why would a man leave his apartment three times on a rainy night with a suitcase and come back three times?" "He likes the way his wife welcomes him home."

Clearly the elision of sex and violence in the film can in part be explained by the MPAA's Production Code, to which *Rear Window* had to conform, and even seems to slyly acknowledge, particularly at the moment when a hovering

Figure 5

helicopter is granted the voyeuristic view of the sunbathers that we are denied. Indeed, the Code required that temporal ellipses be repeatedly used as an aesthetic shorthand for sex in Hollywood films made between roughly 1934 and 1968.[18] It is therefore interesting to consider the way that the film diffuses the potentially problematic suggestion of sexuality during the elided night when Lisa stays over at Jeff's apartment. In theory, it would be very easy for the ellipsis that takes us from Friday night (after Lisa has changed into her nightdress) to Saturday morning (after Stella has joined them) to be used in a manner that suggests Lisa and Jeff have slept together. While Jeff's cast nominally acts to reduce the possibilities for sex, this does not prevent the many allusions made to the sexual implications of Lisa's overnight stay—by Doyle, as well as by Jeff and Lisa—and would thus be unlikely to restrain a viewer's erotic imagination. The possibility for such inferences to be made is sidestepped somewhat, however, by the tone on which the Friday evening scene ends: a dark, violent one, with the discovery of the dead dog and the sinister shot of Thorwald's cigar glowing in the darkness of his apartment. When we fade in again the next morning, Stella has joined the couple and all three are looking intently across at Thorwald's apartment, hypothesizing about how exactly he disposed of his wife's corpse. That this menacing mood is allowed to characterize our sense of the ellipsis effectively banishes thoughts of sex from the spectator's mind, only to replace them with the theme that the film continually links *with* sex through its comparable relationship with elision: violence. That these two themes should be linked at all in the film is an issue necessary of study elsewhere than here (and indeed the close relationship between sex and violence has of course been a recurrent focus of the critical work on Hitchcock's films in general), but we may see that a central way in which they are connected is through the film's uses of ellipsis and occlusion.

Conclusion

In the line from *Rear Window* that inspired this essay's title, Lisa instructs Jeff to "tell me everything you saw, and what you think it means." Bordwell has said that this line "concisely reiterates the film's strategy of supplying sensory information . . . and then forcing Jeff (and us) to interpret it," and furthermore that, in this sense, "every fiction film does what *Rear Window* does."[19] The line is similarly cited by Richard Maltby in *Hollywood Cinema* to help make the point that "when we remember a film we . . . tell ourselves what we saw, and interpret it. The result is a story."[20] It is easy to see why these words might be alluded to in illustrations of the processes by which we understand films, given that they combine the visual, narrated, and interpretive aspects of filmic storytelling and viewing in a pleasingly economical way. If we are truly serious about using the line as a metaphor for the spectator's activity, however, it is worth pointing out that what it does not include is any acknowledgement that what we *don't* see in a film also plays a very important role in our sense of what we "think it means." I hope my preceding discussion has convincingly demonstrated that *Rear Window* itself (and Hitchcock's cinema more generally), by contrast, is very much aware of the importance of the unseen to narrative film.

Rear Window uses ellipses not merely to "skip unimportant intervals," but also to conceal vital portions of story, help establish point of view, convey narrative focus, and reinforce underlying themes. Other forms of elision, particularly what I have termed occlusions, are also used to these and other ends. Focusing on these moments has let us identify some new ways in which Hitchcock achieves several of his characteristic goals and strategies, including suspense, audience misdirection, cognitive alignment, and invocations of the "chaos world." It is probably unsurprising that ellipses can often be made to serve more varied functions than *The Classical Hollywood Cinema*'s schema allows, since (save for the very few films that take place in "real time") the majority of any film's story time will usually have to be elided in one way or another. It is quite possible that Hitchcock's cinema gives ellipses and occlusions special opportunities to assume importance due to his preoccupation with such things as the potential inscrutability of perceptual evidence and the gradual disclosure of perversity beneath the everyday. It also seems plausible that an analysis of the ways the devices operate in other directors' work (or indeed in specific genres or cycles) could prompt useful insights into how exactly they realize *their* particular aesthetic sensibilities and recurring themes. Clearly there is a great deal more work yet to be carried out on this subject, both within Hitchcock's *oeuvre* and beyond.

What must already be evident from my study of one Hitchcock film in isolation, however, is the director's ability to bring a masterful management of the unseen to a story that demands precisely such an approach. The convergence of *Rear Window*'s subject matter with the rhetorical devices used to convey it allows the film to achieve an exceptional synthesis between its themes and style, form and function. In *Film as Film*, V.F. Perkins describes the remarkable stylistic and dramatic unity of *Psycho*'s shower scene, saying that "[Hitchcock] does not let us know whether he has found the style to suit his subject or has found the subject which allows him best exercise of his style." I suggest that we may say the same of *Rear Window*'s ellipses and occlusions, and furthermore that, as Perkins asserts, such a degree of synthesis "represents as well as may be the achievement of any fine filmmaker working at his peak."[21]

Notes

I would like to thank Victor Perkins, James Zborowski, Robert and Sylvia MacDowell, and the editors of the *Hitchcock Annual* for their help in the development of this article.

1. Traditionally, a fade-out/fade-in will tend to be used in "classical" Hollywood cinema to denote a longer temporal elision than a dissolve. While many of the fade-out/fade-ins in *Rear Window* are used to cover transitions spanning a number of hours, or moves between day and night, there are also several that elide what would seem to be periods of less than an hour, e.g., the transition from Jeff and Lisa sitting down to their meal from Twenty One to their later argument, a number of the ellipses during the sequence when Jeff first starts being intrigued by Thorwald's late night trips, and the jump from Lisa entering Jeff's bedroom (in order to change her clothes) to her emerging in her nightdress.

2. Donald Spoto, *The Art of Alfred Hitchcock* (London: W.H. Allen, 1976), 240.

3. Eric Rohmer and Claude Chabrol, *Hitchcock: The First Forty-Four Films*, trans. Stanley Hochman (Oxford: Roundhouse, 1979), 159.

4. David Bordwell, Janet Staiger, and Kristen Thompson, *The Classical Hollywood Cinema: Film Style and Mode of Production to 1960* (London: Routledge, 1985), 44.

5. David Bordwell, *Narration in the Fiction Film* (London: Methuen, 1985), 82.

6. François Truffaut, *Hitchcock* (New York: Simon and Schuster, 1967), 71.

7. Bordwell, *Narration in the Fiction Film*, 82-87.

8. V.F. Perkins, "Where is the World?: The Horizon of Events in Movie Fiction," in John Gibbs and Douglas Pye, eds., *Style and Meaning: Studies in the Detailed Analysis of Film* (Manchester: Manchester University Press, 2005), 26.

9. George Wilson, *Narration in Light: Studies in Cinematic Point of View* (Baltimore: John Hopkins University Press, 1986), 3.

10. Douglas Pye, "Movies and Point of View," *Movie* 36 (2000): 2-34.

11. Valerie Orpen, *Film Editing: The Art of the Expressive*, (London: Wallflower Press, 2003), 42.

12. Quoted in Orpen, *Film Editing*, 33.

13. Later, when Doyle tells Jeff of witnesses' accounts of Thorwald and his wife leaving, Jeff disappointedly says, "6 A.M.? I

think that's about the time I fell asleep," to which Doyle replies, "Too bad: the Thorwalds were leaving their apartment at just that time."

14 Susan Smith, *Hitchcock: Suspense, Humour and Tone* (London: BFI, 2000), 41.

15. For two analyses that, while not dealing specifically with this moment, support these opposed readings of the film's attitude towards Lisa, see Laura Mulvey's "Visual Pleasure and Narrative Cinema," *Screen* 16, no. 3 (1975): 6-18, and Tania Modleski's chapter on *Rear Window* in *The Women Who Knew Too Much: Hitchcock and Feminist Theory* (London: Methuen, 1988), 73-86.

16. Quoted in John Fawell, *Hitchcock's* Rear Window: *The Well-Made Film* (Illinois: Southern Illinois University Press, 2001), 5.

17. Robin Wood, *Hitchcock's Films Revisited*, rev. ed. (London: Columbia University Press, 2002), 84.

18. See Richard Maltby's " 'A Brief Romantic Interlude': Dick and Jane Go to 3½ Seconds of the Classical Hollywood Cinema," in David Bordwell and Noël Carroll, eds., *Post-Theory* (University of Wisconsin Press, 1996), 434-59, and Linda Williams, "Of Kisses and Ellipses: The Long Adolescence of American Movies," *Critical Enquiry* 32, no. 2 (winter, 2006): 288-340 for two detailed discussions of how ellipses can be made to imply sexual activity.

19. Bordwell. *Narration in the Fiction Film*, 42, 46.

20. Richard Maltby, *Hollywood Cinema*, second ed. (London: Blackwell Publishing, 2003), 452. This line is also cited by Wilson at the opening of *Narration in Light*, 1.

21. V.F. Perkins, *Film as Film* (London: Penguin, 1972), 133.

DAVID STERRITT

The Destruction That Wasteth at Noonday: Hitchcock's Atheology

While it is hardly news that the world according to Alfred Hitchcock contains much evil, it is striking to observe what a vast diversity of forms the evil takes: violent crimes, crimes against property, crimes against the state, crimes *of* the state, and an array of miscellaneous misdeeds ranging from unabashed voyeurism to veiled necrophilia. The pervasive presence of so much iniquity, some of it minor but much of it sweepingly malevolent, suggests that Hitchcock sees human beings as habitually prone to what Immanuel Kant terms "radical evil"—the kind of evil that "corrupts the ground" of all subjective moral principles, and which, as a "natural propensity" of humankind, is both inevitable and "*inextirpable* by human powers."[1] Seeing the embrace of radical evil as a form of moral surrender, philosopher Alenka Zupančič defines it as the state of renouncing "the possibility of ever acting [upon] principle" and thus abandoning the very possibility of selfless or disinterested behavior.[2] Along somewhat different lines, legal philosopher Paul W. Kahn observes that Kant's term can designate not only acts and impulses that contravene the law but also evils that are not strictly criminal, such as hatred and jealousy, and those that overwhelm criminal law, such as genocide.[3] Hitchcock's complex view of human nature contained enough skepticism about the notion of innate decency to make him an intuitive researcher into this Kantian version of original sin, and his films abound in both varieties of evil—actions that are illegal in the courtroom sense, such as murder, blackmail, and kidnaping, and actions or attitudes that are iniquitous because of the immorality or injustice they project, such as betrayal, treachery, and deceit. In addition to probing these phenomena through personal and small-group interactions, Hitchcock explored evils that operate beyond the level of individual subjectivity—evils that are embedded in dysfunctional social systems, as in *The Wrong Man* (1956), and in the nature of the fallen world itself, as in *The Birds* (1963).

Far from viewing humankind's capacities for evil from a detached or neutral perspective, moreover, Hitchcock approaches them in ways not dictated but certainly inflected by the Roman Catholic moral teachings that he learned from his religious parents and Jesuit teachers and never fully relinquished. No commentators have seen this more clearly than the pioneering French critics Eric Rohmer and Claude Chabrol, who find Catholic ideas and symbols throughout Hitchcock's work—interpreting the allegorical matrix of *The Wrong Man*, for example, as a denunciation of precisely the moral surrender that Zupančič equates with Kant's radical evil, since the protagonist capitulates during the story to the "theological sins of presumption and despair" and falls prey to "the temptation of diabolical machination," another fundamental Hitchcock theme.[4] Sin, and its close cousin evil, transfixed the director. Arthur Laurents, the screenwriter of *Rope* (1948), commented after Hitchcock's death that it was "obvious to anyone who worked with him that he had a strong sense of sin, and that . . . his Victorian Catholic background . . . affected him deeply."[5] Although his guarded demeanor and ironic temperament precluded much public talk about religion, Hitchcock often contributed money to church-related projects,[6] and in his final days he made a telling remark about his impending death: "One never knows the ending . . . although Catholics have their hopes."[7]

Despite the significance of these themes—the pull of religion and the fascination of incarnate evil—in Hitchcock's work and life, little attention has been given to his films from the standpoint of *theodicy*, the area of philosophy and theology that grapples with the seeming contradiction between the evident presence of evil *in* the world and the putative existence of a benign deity *beyond* the world, drawing conclusions via systematic reasoning (*à la* Gottfried Wilhelm Leibniz and David Hume) rather than the affirmations of tradition and revelation. A theodicy is an effort to "justify the ways of God to men," writes philosopher Alvin Plantinga by way of poet John Milton; more specifically, it is an attempt "to show that God is just in permitting evil," as when (for example) the Free Will Theodicy of St. Augustine calls it a measure of God's goodness

> that He has not refrained from creating even that creature which He foreknew would not only sin, but remain in the will to sin. As a runaway horse is better than a stone which does not run away because it lacks self-movement and sense perception, so the creature is more excellent which sins by free will than that which does not sin only because it has no free will.[8]

My claim in this essay is that Hitchcock's films reveal him as a lay *atheodicist* who uses the expressive-romantic powers of cinema to convey his intuitive sense that by the best evidence of our earthly senses and imaginative minds, belief in a just God whose righteousness nonetheless allows the existence of evil is, to borrow Plantinga's words, "demonstrably irrational or unreasonable."[9]

Engulfing Horror

The horrors of life take many forms, deriving in some instances from indifferent nature and in others from human malefaction, but as philosopher Nick Trakakis points out, "the word 'evil' is reserved in common usage for events and people that have an especially horrific moral quality or character."[10] Theodicy takes on particular interest when the evils at hand are not ordinary or banal but are instead *horrendous*, a term used by philosophers to denote evils so pernicious that participation therein seems, as Marilyn

McCord Adams writes, "prima facie . . . to engulf [or defeat] the positive value of a participant's life," with "participation" meaning that of perpetrator(s) and victim(s) alike.[11] Cultural scholar Philip Tallon takes an intriguing look at this drastic variety of evil in relation to film in his essay "*Psycho*: Horror, Hitchcock, and the Problem of Evil," which posits the central events of the 1960 picture as loci of horrendous evil and asks, among other things, what the justifications might be for Hitchcock's employment of them in a mass-audience movie, or "a *fun* picture," as Hitchcock described it.[12]

I agree with Tallon that *Psycho* is a film "constructed around the horrendous," and that its horrors are not simply a matter of pain and loss but of a grotesque annihilation of existential meaning, wrought by what Augustinian discourse would call the incongruity and disorder that afflict Norman Bates and Marion Crane, albeit in very different ways and to very different degrees.[13] At the same time, though, I agree with Hitchcock that *Psycho* is a fun picture—fun in the gallows-humor sense, not the family-picnic sense—and since I'm not a completely amoral person (or so I like to think), the film's evils and perversities must be significantly less unconscionable than, say, the examples of prototypical horror put forth by Adams, which include cannibalizing one's offspring, slow death by starvation, parental incest, and other such atrocities.[14] *Psycho* would not be a fun picture (by my standards) if it dwelt on loathsome visuals or real profilmic suffering.[15] But it doesn't, and as Hitchcock told me in 1972, he considered this film a comedy; if he'd meant it to be taken as a probing case study, he explained, he would have filmed it straightforwardly (like *The Wrong Man*, perhaps) without ironic or "mysterioso" touches.[16] While calling this chilling film a comedy may overstate the case—when first released it was considered quite disturbing in the sex and violence departments, and many still find it so—its imagery and plot are certainly less horrific than they might have been; the famous shower-murder scene, for instance, hits the audience with so *much* in its split-second montage that very *little* of the mayhem is actually depicted, as Hitchcock never tired of telling interviewers. Then too, in this and other Hitchcock films that depict the horrendous—*Saboteur* (1942) with its murderous fire, *Rope* with its sadistic dinner party, *Torn Curtain* (1966) with the protracted slaying of Gromek, *The Birds* with its chaotic attacks on children—the appalling scenes are woven into narrative frameworks that invite audiences to rationalize, compartmentalize, and thus exorcise the evils on display.

In my view, the Hitchcock scene that most closely approaches the horrendous, if still in a synecdochic and transitory way, occurs in the 1972 thriller *Frenzy*, when the necktie strangler rapes and murders a dating-bureau proprietor who was once married to the film's protagonist. This scene begins when the psychopathic villain patronizes the dating agency and grows wrathful when the broker won't cater to his taste for sadistic sex; although he surely would have killed her whatever she did, it is harshly ironic that by falling under his violent domination she gives him, utterly and tragically against her will, exactly what he demanded. In addition to its visual ferocity, heightened by unsparing closeups, the rape-and-murder sequence takes on great interest in relation to theodicy because its depiction of horrendous evil is counterpointed by words and gestures associated with the ritual of intercessory prayer. Before considering this scene I'll say a bit more about the problem of evil, discuss it briefly in relation to *Psycho*, and consider moments in two earlier Hitchcock films, *The Wrong Man* and *The Birds*, that offer their own insights into the philosophical implications of extreme evil as Hitchcock sees it. Numerous other Hitchcock movies would also serve my purpose, since films from all stages of his career take notice of religion in one way or another—top candidates include *The Lodger* (1927), with its Christological imagery, and *I Confess* (1953), with its morally tormented priest. I might also have chosen the 1934 version of *The Man Who Knew Too Much* for its Tabernacle of the Sun episode; *Shadow of a Doubt* (1943) for its Scripture-quoting killer and vampire-myth allusions; *The Trouble with Harry* (1955) for its fanciful resurrections; *Vertigo* (1958) for its allegorical concern with death and revivification, its pivotal scenes in a church's bell tower, its nuanced references to humanity's fallen state, and other reasons; or *Family Plot* (1976) for its multiple Christian allusions, which gain in resonance by appearing in Hitchcock's only completed film after *Frenzy*, made when his physical and psychological health were in evident decline.[17] But the three films I'll primarily address tap into theodicy-related issues more directly than most of the alternatives, confronting the problem of evil in different ways yet drawing markedly similar conclusions. Their likenesses suggest that the master of suspense was also a master of thematic consistency where this philosophically fraught topos was concerned.

Old, Unanswered Questions

A classic précis of the philosophical problem of evil comes from Hume in his *Dialogues Concerning Natural Religion*, a book-length discussion about the existence of God conducted by three philosophical friends, including one Philo, whose skeptical stances appear to reflect Hume's own outlook. However infinite God's power and wisdom may be, Philo observes, "neither man nor any other animal is happy," and since "the course of Nature tends not to . . . felicity," we must take nature as being "not established for that purpose." These reflections bring to his mind the old, unanswered questions of Epicurus:

> Is he [God] willing to prevent evil, but not able? then is he impotent. Is he able, but not willing? then is he malevolent. Is he both able and willing? whence then is evil?[18]

A good deal of discussion follows, but this formulation sets forth the crux of the issue so straightforwardly that any number of thinkers, up to and including Plantinga and Tallon, have found it a useful reference point for their own arguments on such matters. While it's unlikely that Hitchcock ever read

Hume, it's reasonable to speculate that the filmmaker would have felt some kinship with this philosopher, who was likewise born into a religious environment but "ended his life a refined skeptic who had questioned not only the nature of the world but also the nature of selfhood and, without ever being an atheist, the nature of any belief in God," as film scholar John Orr writes. Hume saw all these things as "human fictions of the most creative sort, but still fictions beyond the complete evidence of the senses," adds Orr, who describes Hume as Hitchcock's "philosophical shadow."[19]

The nature of evil receives one of its most incisive literary discussions in Fyodor Dostoyevsky's novel *The Brothers Karamazov*, where Ivan Karamazov wages great struggles with the problems of pain and suffering. These torment him with particular force in cases where misery afflicts those who are patently innocent of crimes or sins, such as the very young, and the idea that such cases are ultimately justified on some obscure transcendent level does not persuade him. Ivan asks, "If everyone must suffer, in order to buy eternal harmony with their suffering, pray tell me what have children got to do with it? It is quite incomprehensible why they should have to suffer, and why they should buy harmony with their suffering. Why do they get thrown on the pile, to manure someone's future harmony with themselves?" And again, "I absolutely renounce all higher harmony. It is not worth one little tear of even that one tormented child who beat her chest with her little fist and prayed to 'dear God' in a stinking outhouse. . . . I'd rather remain with my unrequited suffering and my unquenched indignation, *even if I am wrong*."[20] Here the skeptical Karamazov brother refuses to accept theodicies that offer the time-tested theological promise of future returns on present agonies; as Michael L. Peterson writes, Ivan believes that "the magnitude of the horrific evils that some tragic human lives include cannot be even approximately estimated without recognizing that they are incommensurate with any collection of goods."[21] This is the kind of evil—of horrendous evil—that Hitchcock examines in the films I look at here, and in so doing he rejects the consolations of theodicy as decisively as Ivan Karamazov did before him.

Although the evils shown in *Psycho* are a shade less darksome than those in some other Hitchcock movies, not to mention those in Ivan's moving lamentation, this film's unflinching gaze at the human capacity for destructive action makes it a good proving ground for the contention that Hitchcock, whose outlook was partially shaped by an orthodox Christian education, came to refute the notion that the horrors of the world are somehow mitigated by greater goods in the last analysis. Not everyone shares my view of Hitchcock as an atheodicist, of course, and Larry E. Grimes takes an opposite tack, arguing that *Psycho* is inscribed in its very first moments (when its Phoenix location and December time period are stated) as an allegory of the phoenix, which is to say rebirth, and of Advent, the season in the Roman Catholic calendar marking Christ's imminent coming. Grimes acknowledges that Marion's murder "heightens the terror of life in the flesh," but he adds that the film ultimately tells us to resist the twin temptations held out by its story—to despair of the human condition, on one hand, or try to resolve the unresolvable, on the other—and instead "live in [our] flesh, know its guilt, its debt, and its death, and watch and wait," because to wait "is to have hope, to adopt a discourse that keeps the life story open." Grimes caps his argument by interpreting the image of Marion's car reemerging from its watery grave as an avowal of the hope for resurrection that is coiled within the "incarnational discourse" of *Psycho* and crystallized in its final image, "which (re)members the body of the film for all who watch and wait without averting their eyes."[22]

Tallon's study of *Psycho* comes to less optimistic conclusions. Contending that horrendous evils are determined less by moral criteria than by aesthetic ones—i.e., their rejection of such classical concepts as proportion and unity in favor of opposite (non)values—he draws on Adams's scholarship to contend that such evils gain their appalling force partly from their capacity for inflicting loss and pain;

partly from their ability to ruin the lives of victims and perpetrators alike; and most of all from the *nature* of the devastation they cause, the physical and *epistemological* destruction brought about by "the disproportion between the amount of moral evil involved and the horrifying results."[23] Tallon then uses *Psycho* to weigh some philosophical responses to the problem of evil. According to the Free Will Defense derived from Augustine, the source of all evil is free will, which is granted by the divine because, as noted earlier, the possibility of making bad choices is a necessary condition for the great benison of authentic relationships with God, angels, and people; in *Psycho*, however, Marion's theft (a moral evil) has little to do with what happens to her once she hits the road out of Phoenix, and the motivations for Norman's murders—to the extent that his motives are explicable at all, and for Hitchcock perhaps they are not— must be rooted less in faulty ethical decisions than in the soul-murdering circumstances of his early life. Verdict: the blessings of free will are far outweighed by the evils depicted in the film. Tallon next cites the argument derived by John Hick from Irenaeus of the early Christian era, averring that evil gives forth suffering that is beneficial for strengthening our characters and our moral intelligence; in *Psycho*, however, lives and minds are flat-out destroyed, not fortified or enriched. Verdict: visiting the Bates Motel is a poor way of building up one's moral fiber.

A third proposition is the Principle of Honesty set forth by Richard Swinburne, who contends that God allows ordinary evils because of their free-will and character-building properties, and also allows gratuitous evils (so called because they could be eliminated with no loss of a corresponding good) since to abolish them would be a sort of divine deceit, foreclosing the benefits we derive from knowing that evil choices have abhorrent consequences. Tallon finds some value here; if theorist Noël Carroll is correct when he hypothesizes that the revulsion we feel toward horrors in cinema is "part of the price to be paid for the pleasure of their disclosure," then perhaps their existence in the world is "part of 'the price to be

Figure 1. Back from the grave in a place of the living dead—Final shot, *Psycho* (1960)

paid' for knowing the truth about evil." Tallon finally concludes, however, that the Principle of Honesty and the price-paid hypothesis provide "at best . . . an incomplete beginning" to rationalizing the problems of evil that *Psycho* so dauntingly poses.[24]

My own view of *Psycho* is closer to that of William Rothman than to that of Tallon and especially to that of Grimes, who cites Rothman's assessment in order to criticize it. "Every film image is a death mask of the world," Rothman writes:

> The world of every film is past. The camera fixes its living subjects, possesses their life. They are reborn on the screen . . . . But life is not fully breathed back into them. They are immortal, but they are always already dead . . . . At the heart of every film is a truth we already know: we have been born into the world and we are fated to die.[25]

Grimes calls this analysis incomplete because it focuses on existential facts without recognizing transcendent possibilities. I find no such incompleteness because Rothman's words, one of the most eloquent threnodies ever composed on a Hitchcock film, accord with my own opinion that while *Psycho* indeed makes its valediction with an image of rebirth (fig. 1), the event is not a hope-full resurrection *à la*

Grimes but rather a stillbirth in a land of the living dead.[26] I see no room here, or in the final obliteration of Norman's selfhood by that of his hallucinated mother, for an Adventitious affirmation of life (re)membered via Christian discourse. *Psycho* may well be "the first film [Hitchcock] made in clear view of his own death," as Rothman has speculated, and there is not a trace of spiritual optimism in its blood-soaked black-and-white frames.[27]

Divine Sarcasm

While the horrendous actions depicted in suspense thrillers like *Psycho* and *Frenzy* are inflicted by individual subjects on individual subjects, *The Wrong Man* approaches the problem of evil from a different, far less personalized perspective. Based on real events, the story centers on Manny Balestrero, a hardworking musician and honest citizen who is arrested, interrogated, and tried for a string of robberies he didn't commit. After humiliation by the police, futile efforts to obtain exculpatory evidence, and a trial almost worthy of Franz Kafka, he is vindicated by the law when a look-alike thief is caught in another crime; but the ordeal has devastated his family, driven his wife Rose literally insane, and taken an undetermined toll on his own mental well-being. Hitchcock follows Hollywood convention (and the real-life story that the film was based on) by adding a final shot of the Balestrero family starting a new life in Florida and a printed text saying that Rose has been "completely cured," but the image is too (deliberately) distant and perfunctory to be persuasive. An unsettling ambiguity also marks the story's key religious moment, which comes when (Every-)Manny prays for strength to get through his tribulations; at this moment the film dissolves from a closeup of his face to that of the "right" man—his name is Daniell, and we haven't seen or heard of him before—on his way to the robbery that gets him arrested and thus resolves the narrative.[28]

This pivotal plot twist can easily be criticized as a sentimental *deus ex machina* device, suggested by the facts of the real-life Balestrero case but clearly dispensable if Hitchcock had wanted a more plausible suspense-picture climax.[29] Close analysis of the prayer scene, however, reveals a serious philosophical skepticism on Hitchcock's part toward Manny's entreaty to the divine.[30] At the beginning of the sequence we see Manny looking at a religious picture— showing Jesus and a star-filled sky—hung on his bedroom wall. Hitchcock cuts to a view of the portrait with Manny's shadow cast alongside it, and then to a closeup of Manny's face, which becomes transparent as Hitchcock superimposes a shot of Daniell walking toward the camera, his face growing to the size of Manny's as he moves into the foreground. This special-effects shot transforms Manny's head into a transparent vessel that the camera methodically fills with another person's form and face, then smoothly obliterates as the superimposition fades and Manny's *doppelgänger* takes over the screen (figs. 2, 3, and 4). What pours into Manny after his prayer is not a transcendent essence of goodness, therefore, but a fearsome specter of the badness that has been tormenting him throughout the film. Manny has prayed for strength, and if the subsequent events are indeed God's response to his supplication, it is a truly sarcastic response: what he receives isn't strength but an external event that gets him off the hook, and what's breathed into him is the vision of a criminal whose antisocial acts have the intensity and potency that his own quest for exoneration, conducted along the pusillanimous lines of his tepid bourgeois life, has disastrously lacked.[31]

Nor can we be absolutely sure that the "right" man is indeed the right man; he is definitely an outlaw who confesses to numerous hold-ups after his arrest, but he might conceivably be just another crook off the street, not the particular bandit for whom Manny has been mistaken by so many people. If we accept this interpretation, at least for the sake of argument, Daniell is another wrong man, another modern Job, another living argument against theodicy. While the injustices that Manny suffers don't approach the ones on Adams's list of horrors, their effects on him, his wife, and his innocent children have the horrific moral quality of which

Figure 2. The *doppelgänger* materializes after Manny's prayer—
Henry Fonda and Richard Robbins, *The Wrong Man* (1956)

Figure 3. The hero and the specter merge

Figure 4. A palimpsest of wrong and right

Trakakis writes, and the agonies they entail are all the more evil because they are born from, cultivated within, and perpetuated by the social system (i.e., the Symbolic Order or Big Other, in the terminology of Jacques Lacan and Slavoj Žižek) that claims to serve and protect, not plague and persecute, its subjects. Trapped beneath that system's crushing amoral weight, neither the wrong man nor the right man has a prayer.

Acts of God

Since the evils inflicted on Manny operate through institutions that hold themselves forth as shields and safeguards *against* evil, and since those evils are facilitated and exacerbated by Manny's own character flaws of submissiveness and diffidence, it is clear that evil requires a definition more expansive than those set down in statutory codes. I've already noted that the category of evil needn't be limited to specifically unlawful acts; as Kahn observes, "there remains an incommensurability, a misunderstanding of the dimensions of the phenomenon, if we are satisfied with the identification of evil as crime."[32] Extending the definition of evil another step, although the word is commonly applied to events and actions with a horrific moral quality rather than to natural processes (earthquakes, floods, fires) that bring about ill consequences, some philosophers find a moral dimension in the latter class as well, arguing that the God who putatively causes or allows cataclysmic "acts of God" may legitimately be judged in moral terms. To support his evidential case for atheism, for instance, William L. Rowe cites the prevalence of intense human and animal suffering that is both inherently abhorrent and self-evidently pointless or gratuitous in the sense discussed above.[33]

The Birds deals directly with God, evil, and the natural world. All three subjects arise in the Tides restaurant and bar after the bird attack at a nearby school.[34] A semi-comical drunk named Jason, described by the screenplay as having "the weary wisdom of booze in him," announces the

Figure 5. Melanie seeks sanctuary amid death and destruction—Tippi Hedren, *The Birds* (1963)

apocalypse in an amusingly chipper tone—"It's the end of the world!"—and then waxes more serious with an apposite passage from the Book of Ezekiel: "'Thus saith the Lord God to the mountains, and to the hills, to the rivers and to the valleys; Behold, I, even I, will bring a sword upon you, and I will destroy your high places.'" Helen, the waitress, laconically tells him that "the Lord's not destroying anything," but Jason persists: "'In all your dwelling places the cities shall be laid waste, and the high places shall be laid waste.' Ezekiel, Chapter 6." The waitress one-ups him without missing a beat: "'Woe unto them that rise up early in the morning that they may follow strong drink,'" but Jason is unfazed, cheerfully identifying her source, "Isaiah, Chapter 5," and repeating his slogan, "It's the end of the world."[35]

This biblical badinage functions largely as comic relief, but the undertones of Old Testament eschatology are far from incidental, and they make a suitably grim prologue for the subsequent scene, in which a bird attack causes a fatal explosion at a gas station and a terrifying interlude for heroine Melanie Daniels as she takes shelter in a telephone booth outside (fig. 5). After this ghastly episode we reenter the Tides, where a group of people aim mournful and accusatory expressions at Melanie and at Hitchcock's camera, as if they were to blame for the story's accumulating catastrophes. Then a young mother in the bar articulates the group's unspoken thoughts.[36] "Who are you?

Figure 6. Mitch and Melanie flee from archetypal disaster—Rod Taylor, Tippi Hedren, *The Birds* (1963)

What are you? Where did you come from?" she ontologically demands, as if Melanie were a devil or a monster instead of merely a newcomer in town. Finally she shrieks the word "evil" in Melanie's face, and Melanie slaps her. The scene ends when Melanie reconnects with Mitch, the movie's hero, and the pair run down a country road toward the recently devastated school, framed amid ground, building, and sky as if they were fleeing an archetypal disaster in some ancient, mythical time (fig. 6).[37]

The Birds takes place in a nihilistic realm where Creation has lost whatever sense it ever had. Evil blossoms from nowhere and from everywhere; incongruity and disproportion reign supreme. It is an elemental film, less concerned with individual human destinies—the characters' fates are unknown at the story's end—than with the rudiments of air, earth, fire, and water as represented by birds, civilization, combustible feelings, and the gulf that separates Bodega Bay from the world at large. It is also a mystical film, punctuated by biblical warnings, besotted jeremiads, and apocalyptic horrors that coincide with the diminishing force of rationality as Mitch's words grow ever more irrelevant and Melanie loses the ability to speak at all. Hitchcock never proffered a more caustic commentary on humanity's helplessness in the face of evils that God either will not or cannot mitigate, if there is a God at all, and the final scene underscores his skepticism in one of the boldest strokes of his career. The protagonists are in severe distress, their antagonists are stronger and more organized than ever, the God of Jason's Bible is nowhere to be found, and now the god of the movie itself abjures his world-making powers in a gesture that Prospero would applaud. The film doesn't resolve, it glides to a conclusion in a breathtaking moment of visual and narrative stasis as the characters creep toward unlikely salvation in some safer, saner place that probably no longer exists. Trying to leave Bodega Bay is the only option they have left, and while their departure may seem to signal faith in a better tomorrow, the near-paralysis imposed by their surroundings is Hitchcock's way of saying that on a planet so terminally out of balance, belief and trust—even trust in his own storytelling powers—are strictly for the birds. If the calamities wrought by the film's eponymous aggressors are acts of God in the insurance-contract sense, metonymic instances of nature's multi-faceted destructiveness, they come from a God that theodicy would find extremely hard to handle. The drunk was wrong: The end of *The Birds* isn't the end of the world, it's the end of *a* world that was human and humane. What the next overlords might make of it we're left to speculate, but judging from the mayhem we've been witnessing, horrendous evil may be entering its golden age.

The Cross and the Psalm

Frenzy, released nine years after *The Birds*, expresses a similarly despairing attitude on a more intimate and realistic scale—no mass attacks, panicked crowds, or ubiquitous and inexplicable villains—that compresses its violence into more concentrated and frightening forms. This film has something of a happy ending, to be sure, as the unwitting alliance of a police inspector and a wrong man gets the right man arrested at the last minute; but this doesn't prevent Hitchcock's atheology from making its most powerful statement of all.

The murders in *Frenzy*, like those in *Psycho*, are organized in a binary structure: Number One is abrupt and explicit, while Number Two replaces graphic representation with muted reference

Figure 7. The cross that Brenda wears against her vulnerable skin—Barbara Leigh-Hunt, *Frenzy* (1972)

to the earlier scene, knowing the viewer's sense memory will fill in the horrendous blanks. The first homicide is the on-screen rape and murder of Brenda Blaney, the entrepreneur of a "marriage and friendship" service; the second is the offscreen rape and murder of Babs Milligan, enacted behind closed doors while the camera retreats downstairs and into a bustling street, indicating that no power or person, including God and the film's godlike director, will intercede on the hapless victim's behalf. As disturbing as Babs's killing is, however, the violation and murder of Brenda is the moment in *Frenzy*, and in Hitchcock's entire *oeuvre*, that most vividly suggests the tension in his mind between a lingering desire for the consolations of traditional religious belief and an intellectual awareness that the world contains unambiguous evils much too prevalent and powerful to be ameliorated, regulated, or even dissimulated by the claims of conventional faith.

In this scene the gods and devils are, as usual, in the details, most notably the cross that Brenda wears around her neck and under her clothing, against her secret and vulnerable skin. The cross is hidden from view as Robert Rusk, the psychotic necktie strangler, commences his attack; we see it for the first time when he tears down the front of her dress, in the same shot where her breasts are first exposed. The visual field then changes, placing the cross outside the frame until a subsequent close-up shows Brenda's hand pulling her brassiere back into place (fig. 7) Then the cross goes invisible

Figure 8. Brenda's last grimace at a horrifying world—
Barbara Leigh-Hunt, *Frenzy* (1972)

again and remains so as the rape concludes, Rusk's psychosis
reaches a frenzied peak, and he strangles Brenda to death in a
series of shots as appalling as any Hitchcock ever crafted. The
next time we see the cross is in the culminating shot of Brenda
lifeless against the casket-like upholstery of her office chair,
vanquished in body and obliterated in spirit; the image's
bilateral symmetry is complete except for the twisted angle of
her speechless tongue, protruding from her mouth in a last
contemptuous grimace at a horrific and horrifying world (fig.
8). The cross lies at the center of her chest, its position in the
frame—dead center on the left-right axis—underscoring the
insensate equilibrium of what was a vital, vigorous being a few
moments before. Gazing at her, we may remember the biblical
passage she spoke while being raped, three verses of Psalm 91:

> Thou shalt not be afraid for the terror by night, nor for
> the arrow that flieth by day; Nor for the pestilence that
> walketh in darkness; nor for the destruction that
> wasteth at noonday; . . . For he shall give his angels
> charge over thee, to keep thee in all thy ways.[38]

After reciting these words she is still until she sees Blaney
start to remove his tie, whereupon she cries, "My God!"
followed seconds later by "Oh Jesus, help me!" These are the

last syllables she is able to gasp before the necktie's stranglehold finishes its work.

Brenda's last words are common ones, of course, and even a committed atheist might utter them in a moment of such traumatizing fear. Still, their presence in this scene is as vital to its meaning as the cross is vital to Brenda's image in death; each of these elements, the psalm and the cross, reinforces the presence and—simultaneously—the utter impotence of the other. The cross gains added retroactive significance, moreover, in a later conversation between Chief Inspector Oxford and his wife, who's questioning him at dinnertime about the big case he's investigating. Told that the killer disposed of the corpse of his latest victim (Babs) by heaving it into the back of a potato truck, and that he returned later to retrieve some damning piece of evidence from the corpse's dead fingers, Mrs. Oxford asks what the crucial object might have been: "a locket? a brooch? a cross?" No, replies the inspector, it would have been something more incriminating—a monogrammed handkerchief, perhaps. Pressed once more about the cross, however, he backpedals: "I don't see why not. Religious and sexual mania are closely linked." Indeed they are, in Hitchcock's dangerous world—but here the linkage is between *Rusk's* sexual mania and *Brenda's* religious hopes, and the bond that connects them is as perilous as it is perverse.

The Grimmest Reaper

Manny Balestrero's prayer in *The Wrong Man*, immediately followed by the revelation and apprehension of the "right" man, is easily taken as a sign of Hitchcock's willingness to accept the idea of a caring, protective God, at least hypothetically or provisionally. Yet the contiguity of these events doesn't affirm a cause-and-effect relationship between them, and as I've suggested, it's not impossible that the stranger who's arrested is another wrong man, the next victim in a cosmic practical joke— offscreen and onscreen, Hitchcock loved practical jokes— perpetrated by the mischievous-malevolent forces of accident, contingency, and chance.[39] *The Birds* is more openly unmoved by spiritual possibilities, picturing an anarchic, entropic world approaching doomsday in a godless, merciless universe. *Frenzy* enacts a more controlled and deliberate argument whose parameters and outcome are never in doubt. Through no fault of her own, the broker of marriage and friendship falls under the shadow of the pestilence which walketh in darkness, embodied by a Covent Garden grocer who slaughters her during lunch hour, munching an apple and croaking the "lovely, lovely" of a mealtime guest presented with a toothsome repast. The man who traffics in English harvests is among the grimmest reapers in all of Hitchcock's cinema.

Hitchcock biographer Donald Spoto has written that from the middle 1940s on, the director's work "became a more acute spiritual autobiography with every film."[40] By this measure *Frenzy*, his penultimate movie, can be considered a privileged index to his philosophy of life (and death) in its most mature and seasoned stage. It is the work that most unambiguously identifies Hitchcock as an atheologian, a thinker whose quarrel with religious systems is based on reasoned acceptance of the premise that a world in which the prayers of a Brenda Blaney go unheard and unheeded is a world in which horrendous evil—the evil that doesn't fortify, convert, or enlighten but merely annihilates, extinguishes, and destroys—is a world in which no benevolent deity can rationally be imagined to exist.

To draw this conclusion about Hitchcock is not to suggest that his atheology was the overriding principle, much less the sum total, of his personal or creative worldview; nor does it mean that he slogged through his days in spiritual despair. Biographies show that he found life well worth living, and many of his films indicate the possibility of contentment, virtue, and moral balance. Yet the biographies also show that Hitchcock suffered from recurring fears and deeply rooted insecurities throughout his life, and a large body of scholarly research and critical interpretation has demonstrated how inextricably his chronic anxieties and existential dreads are woven into the fabric of his art. I conclude, therefore, by returning to the point I made at the beginning of this essay. For all the wit, excitement, and beauty to be found in Hitchcock's cinematic world, it is ultimately a strange and dangerous environment in which evil is pervasively present, multifariously formed, and horrendously unyielding in its defiance of the human values we wishfully call decent, desirable, and right. Hitchcock may have clung to a watered-down Christianity in his personal life—"Catholics have their hopes"—but the unveiling of religion's impotence in his late film *Frenzy* points away from theodicy toward a vision of human experience as ultimately chaotic, unredeemed, and godforsaken.

Notes

Thanks to Sid Gottlieb and Richard Allen for their suggestions and for many great Hitchcock conversations over the years.

1. Immanuel Kant, *Religion Within the Limits of Reason Alone*, trans. Theodore Greene and Hoyt H. Hudson (New York: HarperCollins, 1960), 32. Emphasis in original.

2. Christoph Cox, "On Evil: An Interview with Alenka Zupančič," *Cabinet* 5 (winter 2001/02). <http://www.cabinetmagazine.org/issues/5/alainbadiou. php> accessed 15 February 2008.

3. Paul W. Kahn, *Out of Eden: Adam and Eve and the Problem of Evil* (Princeton: Princeton University Press, 2007), 11. Kahn cites Hannah Arendt, *Eichmann in Jerusalem: A Report on the Banality of Evil* (1964) and Carlos Santiago Nino, *Radical Evil on Trial* (1996).

4. Eric Rohmer and Claude Chabrol, *Hitchcock: The First Forty-Four Films*, trans. Stanley Hochman (New York: Continuum, 1988), 149. French edition, *Hitchcock*, published in 1957.

5. Quoted in Donald Spoto, *The Dark Side of Genius: The Life of Alfred Hitchcock* (Boston: Little, Brown and Company, 1983), 304.

6. Patrick McGilligan, *Alfred Hitchcock: A Life in Darkness and Light* (New York: ReganBooks, 2003), 440.

7. Spoto, *Dark Side of Genius*, 554-55.

8. Alvin Plantinga, *God, Freedom, and Evil* (Grand Rapids: William B. Eerdmans, 1974), 27. The passage by St. Augustine comes from *The Problem of Free Choice*, vol. 22 of *Ancient Christian Writers* (Westminster: The Newman Press, 1955), Bk. 2, 15; Milton's words come from *Paradise Lost*, second ed. (London: S. Simmons, 1674), 4:26. A theodicy is different from a "defense," because while a theodicist tries to decide what God's reason *is* for permitting evil, a defender tries to set forth, as Plantinga puts it, "at most what God's reason *might possibly be*" (28, emphasis in original).

9. Plantinga, *God, Freedom, and Evil*, 3.

10. Nick Trakakis, "The Evidential Problem of Evil," in *The Internet Encyclopedia of Philosophy* <http://www.iep.utm.edu/e/evil-evi.htm> accessed 1 March 2008.

11. Marilyn McCord Adams, "Horrendous Evils and the Goodness of God," in Marilyn McCord Adams and Robert Merrihew Adams, eds., *The Problem of Evil* (Oxford: Oxford University Press, 1990), 209-21, cited at 211. See also Marilyn McCord Adams, "The Problem of Hell: A Problem of Evil for Christians," in William L. Rowe, ed., *God and the Problem of Evil* (Malden: Blackwell, 2001), 282-309, especially 285.

12. Philip Tallon, "*Psycho*: Horror, Hitchcock, and the Problem of Evil," in David Baggett and William A. Drumin, eds., *Hitchcock and Philosophy: Dial M for Metaphysics* (Chicago: Open Court, 2007), 49-61. Hitchcock's words are from Ian Cameron and V.F. Perkins, "Hitchcock," *Movie* 6 (January 1963): 4-6; reprinted in Sidney Gottlieb, ed., *Alfred Hitchcock: Interviews* (Jackson: University Press of Mississippi, 2003), 44-54, cited at 47; quoted in Tallon, "*Psycho*," 49.

13. Tallon, "*Psycho*," 51, 61.

14. Adams, "Horrendous Evils and the Goodness of God," 211-12.

15. Movies like *Cannibal Holocaust* (Ruggero Deodato, 1980) and the *Faces of Death* pictures (John Alan Schwartz, 1978-90) are as far removed from Hitchcock's aesthetics as films can be.

16. Quoted in David Sterritt, *The Films of Alfred Hitchcock* (Cambridge: Cambridge University Press, 1993), 113.

17. For more on this aspect of *Family Plot*, see David Sterritt, "Alfred Hitchcock: Registrar of Births and Deaths," *Hitchcock Annual*, 1997-98; reprinted in Sidney Gottlieb and Christopher Brookhouse, eds., *Framing Hitchcock: Selected Essays from the* Hitchcock Annual (Detroit: Wayne State University Press, 2002), 310-22.

18. David Hume, *Dialogues Concerning Natural Religion* (Stilwell: Digireads.com, 2006), 42. A bit later Philo asks why there should be "any misery at all in the world" and continues, "Is it from the intention of the Deity? But he is perfectly benevolent. Is it contrary to his intention? But he is almighty" (43-44). To be fair to Philo, in these passages he is making a case against anthropomorphic notions of deity, asking whether God's "benevolence and mercy [may be taken to] resemble the benevolence and mercy of men" in light of the fact that the "curious artifice and machinery" bestowed on living things have no object other than the "preservation alone of individuals, and propagation of the species . . . without any care or concern for the happiness" thereof; whether mystical conceptions of God may be valid gives rise to different questions.

19. John Orr, *Hitchcock and Twentieth-Century Cinema* (London: Wallflower Press, 2005), 27, 134.

20. Fyodor Dostoyevsky, *The Brothers Karamazov*, trans. Richard Pevear and Larissa Volokhonsky (New York: Farrar, Straus and Giroux, 2002), 244-45 (emphasis in original). Adams, in "Horrendous Evils and the Goodness of God," places "child abuse of the sort described by Ivan Karamazov" on her list of paradigmatic horrendous evils.

21. Michael L. Peterson, *God and Evil: An Introduction to the Issues* (Boulder: Westview Press, 1998), 124.

22. Larry E. Grimes, "Shall These Bones Live? The Problem of Bodies in Alfred Hitchcock's *Psycho* and Joel Coen's *Blood Simple*," in Joel W. Martin and Conrad E. Ostwalt, Jr., eds., *Screening the Sacred: Religion, Myth, and Ideology in Popular American Film* (Boulder: Westview Press, 1995), 19-29, cited at 23-24, 25

23. Tallon, "*Psycho*: Horror, Hitchcock, and the Problem of Evil," 57.

24. Tallon, "*Psycho*: Horror, Hitchcock, and the Problem of Evil," 61. The quoted words appear in Noël Carroll, *The Philosophy of Horror or Paradoxes of the Heart* (New York: Routledge, 1990), 184.

25. William Rothman, *Hitchcock — The Murderous Gaze* (Cambridge: Harvard University Press, 1982), 1; quoted in Grimes, "Shall These Bones Live?," 28. This passage is strongly influenced by André Bazin's writing on the ontology of the photographic image.

26. Norman's zombie-like state in the penultimate scene, I've written, "is universalized in the final shot of the film, when the toilet-swamp becomes a birth site, delivering up Marion's corpse . . . umbilically connected to Hitchcock's camera and the world beyond" (Sterritt, *The Films of Alfred Hitchcock*, 117).

27. Rothman, *Hitchcock — The Murderous Gaze*, 341.

28. Marshall Deutelbaum claims that "the real thief is often visible in the film as he and Balestrero cross paths," but Bill Krohn rebuts this, stating that according to production records, the actor who plays Daniell wasn't on the set when the shots Deutelbaum adduces were filmed. See Marshall Deutelbaum, "Finding the Right Man in *The Wrong Man*," in Marshall Deutelbaum and Leland Poague, eds., *A Hitchcock Reader* (Ames: Iowa State University Press, 1986, 207-18, cited at 216; and Bill Krohn, *Hitchcock at Work* (London: Phaidon, 2000), 180.

29. Deutelbaum reports that although the real Balestrero was a "religious man" who prayed during his trial, he was "not praying, but playing in the Stork Club band" when police made the arrest that cleared his name ("Finding the Right Man in *The Wrong Man*," 210).

30. For more on this, see David Sterritt, *"The Wrong Man,"* in Mary Lea Bandy and Antonio Monda, eds., *The Hidden God: Film and Faith* (New York: The Museum of Modern Art, 2003), 94-99.

31. For discussion of Manny as guilty, see Sterritt, *The Films of Alfred Hitchcock*, 65-81.

32. Kahn, *Out of Eden*, 11.

33. That is to say, "an omnipotent, omniscient being [i.e., the God of orthodox theism] could have prevented [it] without thereby losing some greater good or permitting some evil equally bad or worse." William L. Rowe, "The Problem of Evil and Some Varieties of Atheism," in Marilyn McCord Adams and Robert Merrihew Adams, eds., *The Problem of Evil*, 126-37, cited at 127.

34. Screenplay quotations are taken from the version identified as "Final Draft/2nd Revision/March 2, 1962" and posted on *Drew's Script-O-Rama* www.script-o-rama.com/movie_scripts/b/the-birds-script-screenplay.html.

35. Jason is quoting Ezekiel 6:3, 6 (not quite accurately; most translations give "high places shall be desolate" rather than "laid waste") and Helen is quoting Isaiah 5:11.

36. She is played by Doreen Lang, who had made her feature-film debut as one of Manny's accusers in *The Wrong Man*.

37. For further discussion of this moment, see Sterritt, *The Films of Alfred Hitchcock*, 119-43, especially 134-37.

38. Psalms 91:5, 6, 11 in the King James translation.

39. I'm not asserting that Daniell is *probably* another "wrong" man and I'm not arguing that Hitchcock purposely made this issue ambiguous; what I do suggest is that Hitchcock had a strong affinity for ambiguities of many kinds, and that this predilection might explain why the *possibility* that Daniell is another "wrong" man is not entirely foreclosed. On the general point that the conclusion of *The Wrong Man* is "obviously ambiguous," see Rohmer and Chabrol, who state that "a certain freedom of judgment is left us" *vis-à-vis* the apparent miracle of Daniell's arrest; that "we are permitted to *believe in the possibility* of [another] miracle" *vis-à-vis* Rose's chances for recovery (my italics); and that the ambiguous ending "is no hedge: the ambiguity is in things themselves. It is characteristic of Hitchcock to show us both sides of the coin" (*Hitchcock*, 148-49). I refer precisely to the two sides of that ontological coin. For more on Hitchcockian ambiguity, see Sterritt, "Alfred Hitchcock: Registrar of Births and Deaths," 310-11.

40. Spoto, *Dark Side of Genius*, 274.

GRAIG UHLIN

Gus Van Sant's Mirror-Image of Hitchcock: Reading *Psycho* Backwards

Gus Van Sant's shot-by-shot remake of Alfred Hitchcock's *Psycho* (1960) is not unprecedented in the history of film remakes. John Cromwell's *Algiers* (1938), an American remake of the French film *Pépé le Moko* (Julien Duvivier, 1937) reproduces many of the same camera set-ups as the original, as well as literally poaching documentary footage from the French version (the American distributor bought all the copies of *Pépé le Moko* in distribution).[1] At the advent of the sound era, multiple versions of the same film were shot simultaneously in order to target foreign markets while saving production costs. For instance, Hitchcock's German-language *Mary* (1931) is a remake of the his British film *Murder!* (1930)—the two films were shot at the same time using a different set of actors. More recently, filmmaker Michael Haneke released a shot-by-shot English-language remake (with an American cast) of his 1997 film, *Funny Games*. In these cases, the shot-by-shot fidelity to the original is justified by a film's distribution outside its country of origin. For Van Sant's remake, the justification is based not on national boundaries but on a generational divide. Van Sant remarked that he intended to introduce Hitchcock's classic to a generation of younger viewers who may have heard of the film and its surprising plot twists, but had never actually seen it. This justification failed, however, to convince an entire generation of critics, who considered Van Sant's film to be nothing less than heretical.

In the criticism surrounding Van Sant's remake of Hitchcock's *Psycho*, there has been an effort to discriminate between the two directors. Commentators unsympathetic to the remake seek to separate out the "good" Hitchcock from the "bad" Van Sant, while more sympathetic critics want to allow room for defending Van Sant's film as more than a "degraded copy" or poor imitation of the masterful original work. For instance, Paula Marantz Cohen argues that Van Sant's film constitutes "the consummate homage to the Master" and a commendable "hybrid of art and criticism."[2] Constantine Verevis points out that Van Sant's version cannot be understood outside the numerous other imitations of Hitchcock's classic film, including its sequels and references to the film by contemporary Hollywood directors such as Brian de Palma.[3] He cites Douglas Gordon's art-installation piece *24-Hour Psycho*, which exhibits Hitchcock's film unchanged except for its projection speed (slowed to two frames per second), and argues that Van Sant's film, like Gordon's museum piece, produces a unique and singular experience (an "absolute difference") even as it repeats the original film exactly.

Van Sant's remake, however, is not simply a new event, maintaining an "absolute difference" from the original. Its shot-by-shot fidelity makes it a re-creation of the original. While Gordon's art-installation piece alters the conditions of exhibition of the original, the film itself remains the same. The slowed projection speed opens a new way of experiencing the familiar film, as the snail's pace of its progression disrupts the suspense of the narrative and turns the attention of the viewer to the details of the image, often gone from the screen too quickly to take in. Since Van Sant's *Psycho* actually remakes the original film, unlike Gordon's piece, it produces not just a different viewing position marked by a fetishistic and critical attachment to the original, but also one marked by innocence and earnestness. In other words, the spectator of the Van Sant's film is offered two different viewing positions. One can approach the film "innocently," as one would have watched the original, where all the elements of suspense and intrigue hold firm. This respects Van Sant's intention of introducing the film to a new generation of viewers. However, one can also view Van Sant's *Psycho* as a critical and self-aware spectator who, attuned to Van Sant's postmodern approach to the remake as simulacrum or copy that seeks to reproduce the original, searches for the elements that differentiate it. This knowing spectator, as opposed to the imagined naïve one of a new generation, practices the same critical procedures produced by Gordon's piece, except now the obsessive attention to the details of the image is directed toward enumerating the differences between Van Sant's film and the original.

On the one hand, the viewer may watch the film "straight," letting oneself be guided by the narrative momentum, where all of Hitchcock's intended shock effects still work, at least potentially. This "naïve" spectatorial position may actually be an impossible one. As Thomas Leitch observed, many of those critical of the remake held the film up to the standard of recreating the original experience of Hitchcock's film. He writes, however, that "the experience that made their first viewing of *Psycho* such an unforgettable experience for so many audiences of a certain age is no longer available to most contemporary audiences, who are necessarily watching the film through a host of intertexts Verevis has noted."[4] Thus, there are no more "innocent" viewers of Hitchcock's film—not even if they are actually watching Hitchcock's film. Leitch suggests that:

> Just as watching Van Sant can never give us more than something like the experience of watching Hitchcock, neither can the experience of watching Hitchcock, because every reading and every viewing of Hitchcock's film is not only different from every other but is defined by those differences.[5]

Yet Van Sant's claim to introduce the film to a new generation trades on this possibility; it presumes a spectator who does not, as it were "know enough."

On the other hand, Van Sant's remake is also subtly directed at the Hitchcock enthusiast, to a spectator characterized by a cinephilic attachment to the original. This is the spectator presumed to "know too much," whose repeated viewings of Hitchcock's film will be rewarded by a close, attentive engagement with Van Sant's re-creation. This spectatorial experience is a form of what Patricia White has called "retrospectatorship," where the reception of a film is informed by "unconscious and conscious past viewing experience."[6] With retrospectatorship, the interaction between film and spectator is not a "first encounter." Rather, as with contemporary viewings of classical Hollywood films, a viewer's reception of the film is influenced by extratextual sources, including social community, individual identity, and marketing and publicity discourses. White examines how a contemporary lesbian viewing subject "revises" Joseph Mankiewicz's film, *All About Eve* (1950), encoding a lesbian seduction fantasy into its story of one woman's (Eve) unyielding devotion to another (Margo Channing). Retrospectatorship names the different vantage point assumed when one views a historically distant text within a new film-going context. Here, the meaning of the film is not limited to the text but also extends to the accumulated connotations a film has received since its release. For this critical, self-aware spectator, attention is deflected away from following the narrative—there are no surprises in store for this viewer—and redirected toward a careful scanning of the image for details and marginal features of the text. This viewer is less concerned with following the story and anticipating what happens next than with the discontinuities between Hitchcock's film and Van Sant's re-creation. Consider, for instance, Thomas Leitch's "101 Ways to Tell Hitchcock's *Psycho* from Van Sant's," which enumerates small deviations between the two texts, and thus bears witness to both a fetishistic attachment to the original and a rewarding critical exercise that demonstrates an attentive eye to detail.[7] As Esther Anatolitis makes clear, Van Sant's atypical film reverses the usual procedure by which one engages a film and its remake by forcing one to look for "differences within a field of repetition."[8]

Preserving Mother, Preserving Psycho

These two spectatorial positions, which may be occupied by a single spectator, describe the split viewing position produced by Van Sant's shot-by-shot remake. This splitting of the self originates from within Hitchcock's film. That is to say, Van Sant reproduces the thematic content of Hitchcock's film at the level of form, literalizing and exteriorizing the repressed content of the original—namely, Norman's split personality, revealed finally only in the last scenes. Through a careful control over the film's narrative and *mise-en-scène*, using techniques such as voice-off and selective framing, Hitchcock suppresses the viewer's knowledge of Norman's identity, his psychological incorporation of his mother's personality into his own. While for Van Sant's remake this suppression of knowledge was not impossible (assuming that there is actually a generation of viewers who not only had never seen the film but also never encountered references to it within popular culture), he keeps open the possibility of more nuanced reception that consistently takes into account the viewer's familiarity with the film.

The shot-by-shot fidelity of the remake makes one feel as if he or she is watching the same object but from a different vantage point, from some unfamiliar viewing position. This position is one where the viewer is asked to watch the film backwards, so to speak, where the retroactive knowledge of the original film's suppressed content is always operative. Thus, the surprise or suspense of watching the remake is not eliminated entirely, but it is reduced as one's attention is deflected away from the hermeneutic questions toward stylistic features and smaller details in the text. And it is this spectatorial response—evidenced no doubt by the obsessive critical desire to separate "bad" Van Sant from "good" Hitchcock—that perhaps explains why Van Sant resorted to the "stunt" of a shot-by-shot re-creation, and why he chose *Psycho* in the first place. After all, why not remake *Vertigo* (1958) or *Rear Window* (1954), which are no less iconic representations of Hitchcock's body of work?

I would suggest that Van Sant's film literally enacts Norman's (failed) preservation of the lost love object. Just as Norman seeks to maintain the illusion that his mother is living, so too does Van Sant seek to resuscitate a "dead" classic—at least insofar as he imagines a generation of viewers to be ignorant of it. In both instances, cosmetic upkeep serves to mask an irreparable loss, and manipulation of the surface (e.g., wigs, use of color film stock) serves, however unsuccessfully, to return the lost object to its living form, to restore it to the present, while at the same time keeping it exactly the same. And in both cases, as circumstances demand, the "child" must literally take the place of the lost "parent." Thus, the preservative impulse *of* Van Sant's film has its origins in the preservative impulse *in* Hitchcock's. Unlike other remakes that have to make a trade-off between fidelity to the spirit of the text or fidelity to its form, Van Sant's film is faithful to the essence of the original precisely by being faithful to its letter. It is only by literally embodying or reenacting Norman's psychosis, by transferring from content to form, that Van Sant is able to be faithful to the representation of it.

The alignment of this spectatorial position with Norman's character has its origin in Hitchcock's film. Indeed, it completes the shift in identification begun by Hitchcock: when he killed off his heroine, Hitchcock left his viewers to attach their desire for identification to the only character available, Norman. Van Sant's film replays Hitchcock's original from the perspective of Norman—not literally through a different use of point-of-view shots, for instance, but through the production of an alternative reading strategy that continually inflects the meaning of the film thanks to our awareness of what happens in the film. Thus, unlike with Hitchcock's film, we may not even identify with Marion's character; instead, as experienced viewers of horror film conventions, firmly established in the wake of the original *Psycho*, we regard her as a surveilled and vulnerable object. Our position, then, is potentially always aligned with Norman even before he appears in the remake. His psychosis and split-personality structure and determine the spectatorial responses to Van Sant's film.

One such symptom of Norman's psychosis that we witness in Hitchcock's film that is also exhibited in the Van Sant remake is the desire to maintain original conditions. As Lila searches the Bates house, the viewer becomes aware that his mother's bedroom is preserved exactly (we presume) as it had been at the time of her death, her clothes and belongings dutifully in their place. The mattress bears the deep impression where she (or Norman, in her place) would sleep. Norman's own childhood bedroom is maintained exactly as it was, with the toys and other children's items strewn about, though with the addition of a book whose hidden content we take to be pornographic. The implications are clear: Norman's mental development has stalled, as he continually lives his life through the memory of a more idyllic past even as time continues moving forward in the outside world. Van Sant's remake embodies this same paradoxical temporality. The choice to update the material to the 1990s only emphasizes how the film feels stuck in the 1960s, miming Norman's own fervent attachment to the past. Like Norman, the film can "tinker at the edges" (e.g., the Walkman, Viggo Mortensen's nudity) in attempting to give the remake a "lifelike" presence, a contemporary look, but nothing is going to be sufficient to mask the death at its center, the temporal stasis at its core. Norman's own perverse incorporation of his mother's identity is repeated by Van Sant as the perverse incorporation of Hitchcock's film: both are an obsessive attempt to resuscitate the "corpse" of the lost object. The persistence of the cultural memory of Hitchcock's film—its frequent appearance within American popular culture—is accompanied by a corresponding restoration of the physical body (of the film), just as the virtual life of Norman's mother is matched by the literal preservation of her body.

The Mirror Image

The idea that one experiences the original "backwards"—at least potentially, as one part of a split spectatorial response to the film—manifests itself visually in the remake. The cinephilic viewer, freed from the necessity of following the plot, may turn his or her attentive eye to the details of the image, where Van Sant has visually inscribed the notion that the remake is not simply a literal reproduction of the original but its mirror image. While many of the differences between the two films result simply from the impossibility of the project—Van Sant's film could not possibly perfectly replicate the décor and elements of the *mise-en-scène* from the earlier film—there are purposeful deviations that are subtle but important. Specifically, Van Sant repeatedly—and seemingly for no discernible reason or limitation imposed by shooting on location—reverses the screen direction from the original. For instance, in the point-of-view shot of the Bates house, seen by Marion when she first arrives at the motel, Van Sant has the silhouetted figure in the window, representing Norman's mother, walk from right to left across the window, while in the original, she walks left to right (figs. 1a and 1b).

There are no restrictions that would have dictated Van Sant make this change, other than a desire that his film be perceived as the mirror image of Hitchcock's. This is not an isolated instance; rather, it is one example of a recurring motif. For example, in the scene where Marion trades in her car for another, Van Sant twice reverses screen direction from what it is in Hitchcock's version, first when Marion talks with the salesman and second when she buys a newspaper to see if there is any news of her theft (figs. 2a and 2b, 3a and 3b). Likewise, when Arbogast phones to offer an update on his investigation, he faces screen left, his face slightly angled toward the camera, a positioning that flips Hitchcock's original (figs. 4a and 4b). Finally, in one image from the montage of Arbogast's investigation, Van Sant preserves the diagonal line of Hitchcock's blocking (from top-left to bottom-right), but by exploiting the relative heights of his actors, reverses their positions as well as the placement of the "Rooms for Rent" sign (figs. 5a and 5b).

Figs. 1a and 1b. The silhouetted figure of Norman's mother passes across the window of the Bates home in Alfred Hitchcock's *Psycho* (1960) and Gus Van Sant's *Psycho* (1998). In this and all subsequent figures, I place the frame-capture from Hitchcock's film above the image from Van Sant's remake.

Figs. 2a and 2b. Marion Crane (Janet Leigh, above, and Anne Heche, below) trades in her car at an auto dealership.

Figs. 3a and 3b. Marion Crane buys a newspaper to check for news of her theft.

Figs. 4a and 4b. Investigator Milton Arbogast (Martin Balsam, above, and William H. Macy, below) makes a phone call from the Bates Motel.

Figs. 5a and 5b. Gus Van Sant revises Hitchcock's blocking of Arbogast's investigation.

Van Sant also occasionally inverts the image through a change in the blocking of the actors, shifting their placement within the background and foreground of the frame, or through a point-of-view shot that flips the image vertically perpendicularly, reversing the frame on an up-down axis. In the first example, where the reversal is lost somewhat in still images, Hitchcock uses a backward tracking shot that begins in Sam Loomis's office and terminates once it picks up the old woman and the shop clerk (fig. 6a). In the Van Sant version (fig. 6b), there is a similar tracking shot, though the camera pivots as it leaves the office, and tracks forward rather than backward. The old woman, further, steps into the frame, rather than the frame picking her up through its movement, and she does it from the other direction than in Hitchcock's film. In a second example (figs. 7a and 7b), Van Sant places his camera on the side of Norman's mother's bed opposite to Hitchcock's camera position, such that the image is no longer seen from Lila's point-of-view. In a third example (figs. 8a and 8b), Van Sant both switches the positioning of his actors (moving Norman from the foreground to the background) and, unlike the example shown in figures 5a and 5b, changes the diagonal line created by Hitchcock (which now goes from top-left to bottom-right, instead of the reverse). By doing so, Van Sant makes Norman seem more threatening and dominant, rather than vulnerable and passive.

Pop Psycho

These remarkable but subtle deviations from the original film, barely noticeable to a viewer who is not able to view the two films side by side, put Van Sant's film in a lineage of appropriation, sometimes literal, initiated by Dadaism and carried out to its fullest extent by Pop Art. Leitch likens the shot-by-shot reproduction of the original to Andy Warhol's Campbell's soup cans, first exhibited in 1962. Warhol famously appropriated the images of commodity culture— including the soup cans, life-sized replicas of Elvis Presley or cropped photographs of Marilyn Monroe and Jacqueline

Figs. 6a and 6b. While Hitchcock uses a backward tracking movement in this scene, Van Sant's camera tracks forward.

Figs. 7a and 7b. The position of the indentation of Norman's mother's body in Hitchcock's film is reversed in Van Sant's.

Figs. 8a and 8b. Gus Van Sant exploits the relative heights of his actors (Vince Vaughn, left, and Viggo Mortensen) to change the blocking of Hitchcock's original staging.

Kennedy, and Brillo detergent boxes—placing them within a high-art context. The neo-Dada gesture, reprising Marcel Duchamp's ready-mades, effectively erased the divide between high and low culture, not to mention fine art and commercial art. Unlike other pioneers of the Pop Art movement, including Robert Rauschenberg and Jasper Johns, Warhol made no distinction between his commercial artistic practice and his fine-art aspirations (Warhol was the most successful commercial illustrator in New York during the period directly preceding his famous Campbell's Soup Can exhibition at the Ferus Gallery in Los Angeles). Warhol's own cinematic practice, moreover, extended his Pop Art aesthetic into a new medium, as his early silent films—most notably, *Empire* (1964)—were engaged in a theatricalization of the everyday ("The Empire State Building is a star!" he said). These films featured a characteristic use of repetition (*Empire*, for instance, consists of an eight-hour static shot of the Empire State Building) as the viewer is confronted with a nearly unchanging image for an extended duration, or alternatively with serialized repetitions on a single theme (the weekly installments of *Kiss*, for instance, consist of a different couple kissing for a full three minutes).

Warhol, not surprisingly, has been a strong influence on Van Sant's filmmaking practice. The director had plans, which never materialized, to direct a biopic of the Pop artist, starring River Phoenix. Previous to that, when Van Sant attended the Rhode Island School of Design, where he (like Warhol) studied painting before becoming a filmmaker, Warhol was the dominant influence on young artists of his generation. "At RISD, everyone was into fame, that was a Warholian thing," Van Sant has said.[9] Critic Amy Taubin has drawn the connections between the two filmmakers perhaps more than anyone. She cites references to Warhol's cinema in Van Sant's work—including an homage to *Blow Job* (1964) in *My Own Private Idaho* (1991), as the camera lingers in close-up on Phoenix's face as he is being fellated. The quirky johns in the hustling scenes of that film—one of which involves Warhol superstar Udo Kier—recall the oddball men who pick up Joe Dallesandro in *Flesh* (1968).

The kind of repetition and appropriation found in Warhol's work is likewise seen across the entirety of Van Sant's filmmaking career. The director famously incorporated portions of Shakespeare's *Henry IV* into *My Own Private Idaho*, using the Hal-Falstaff relationship of the play to structure his own narrative about Scott Favor's renunciation of his street-father Bob. The appropriation of Shakespeare entails a similar operation that informs Van Sant's remake of *Psycho*—the placement of a canonical, classic text into a low-class context (here, the milieu of street hustlers in Portland, Oregon). Once again, Van Sant was thought to "degrade" the culturally sanctified original, parasitically exploiting it for its high-art connotations and using it toward "deviant" ends. There are numerous other examples of appropriation to be found in Van Sant's work: the use of real-life stories as source material (*To Die For* [1995], loosely based on the case of Pamela Smart, who was convicted of hiring three high-school students to kill her husband; *Elephant* [2003], based on the Columbine murders; *Last Days* [2005], based on the suicide of Kurt Cobain); the stylistic imitation of Bela Tarr in Van Sant's *Gerry* (2002), which literally restages several shots from the Hungarian director's *Satantango* (1994); and the recurring use of Western motifs and iconography. Apart from the *Psycho* remake, moreover, the director purposely repeats his earlier works. He acknowledges that *Finding Forrester* (2000) is little more than a reiteration of his earlier box-office hit, *Good Will Hunting* (1997)—"I think I thought because [*Finding Forrester*] wasn't that different from something I'd done before, that in itself was different"[10]—and the "Death Trilogy" (which encompasses *Gerry*, *Elephant*, and *Last Days*) features a similar aesthetic style (long takes, nonchronlogical time line, minimal action) focused around a central murder.

The connection between Warhol's Pop aesthetics and Van Sant's remake is frequently made on the basis of this use of repetition, which minimizes the differences between an original and its copies. Warhol's screenprints and early films replicate commodity and pop-culture images without altering them, presenting his viewer with soup can as soup can, or

Empire State Building as itself, redirecting the viewer's attention to their own spectatorial investment in the artwork and the institutional context that grants its aesthetic, cultural, and monetary value. Warhol no doubt hoped to provoke just such a response to his work as occurred at the first exhibition of his Soup Cans when a grocery store down the street from the gallery mockingly advertised in their window that customers could get the real thing for just thirty-three cents. His work challenged the appearance of value that was supposed to accrue from a fine-art institutional context, as he sought a radical democratization of art (what he called "commonism") that refused any hierarchy or stinginess in the distribution of cultural or aesthetic prestige. As he put it, more succinctly, "everything is pretty."

Like Warhol, Van Sant's remake seeks to minimize the differences between the original and its copy, at least insofar as his stated intention goes, but not, as we have already noted, without changes that are both strategic (e.g., new blocking of actors, color) and forced by circumstances (e.g., new actors). Such changes were not alien to Warhol either. While his works copied their originals, he embellished and changed various aspects of them. The screenprints add color (e.g., Gold Marilyn, Green Marilyn) while the early silent films were projected at silent speed, though they were shot at sound speed, resulting in an almost imperceptible distending of time. These small embellishments (Warhol's own "tinkering at the edges") removed the works from any simple mundane reproduction of reality, forcing the spectator to cast off his or her sedimented view of the banal, everyday object depicted (something that may not even garner a second look normally) and encounter it anew, either to see reality transformed without the accretions of its cultural baggage or to prove the inexhaustible charisma of the star- or commodity-image.

Intimations of Van Sant's own project are to be found here, as his stated interest in introducing Hitchcock's film to new audiences entailed a literal reproduction of the original that required its viewer to look at it anew, from a different vantage point. After all, Warhol's minimal and repetitive images resisted spectatorial absorption, redirecting the viewer's attention to the surface of the work (the instant recognizability of the logo or star image, the grain of the film stock or gradations of light projected through the celluloid) and to their own spectatorial investment in the art object. These conscious changes, moreover, were accompanied by equally as important unintentional ones, such as the accidental splatterings of ink with each successive screenprint of the same image. Thus, even as the viewer is confronted with the repetition of the same image—whether of Marilyn Monroe or the Empire State Building—Warhol forced that viewer to look for, just as has been observed of Van Sant's remake, "differences within a field of repetition," reversing the usual procedure by which one engages with a film and its remake (where one would look for continuities between two texts, not discontinuities).

Authorship as Self-Erasure

Authorship is traditionally defined as the unique and creative "signature" or identifiable style of the artist as it is expressed in the work. Critics thus seek to identify Van Sant's authorship in his deviations from Hitchcock's original film. Steven Jay Schneider, for instance, makes the case that the remake can be understood as a "Van Sant film" given its thematic and formal similarities to earlier Van Sant works, including the use of nondiegetic inserts to represent heightened emotional experience.[11] Yet it is this procedure that Van Sant (not unlike Warhol before him) seeks to disrupt by relocating the trace of his authorship in the exact reduplication of the object—that is, within imitation and sameness. Warhol consistently sought to erase his authorship internally within the work even as he sought to retain it in a Duchampian mode, as the signature (or for Warhol, the autograph) that denominates the text as his own, retroactively as it were, and not as the result of his own creative involvement in the work (the production of which may indeed have been delegated to some other laborer). Thus, early in his fine-art career, Warhol abandons expressionistic brushstrokes in favor a cold, hard line that betrays no aspect of the artist's personality. Then, when he begins making films, he opts to abdicate directorial responsibility to the movie camera itself, often turning it on and walking away from it, letting contingent elements determine his *mise-en-scène*. In this way, he develops and perpetuates his desire to become a machine, for art to be purely mechanical, turning creative production into mechanical reproduction (which is what Van Sant does, by "reverse-engineering" Hitchcock's film, as if following a tracing pattern). Further, late in his film career, when Paul Morrissey had assumed near-total control over the Factory's cinematic output, Warhol asserts his own name as brand ("Andy Warhol Presents"), completing the transformation of his own persona into pure image.

Like Warhol, Van Sant has consistently worked to disrupt conventional notions of authorship, and the institutional and critical contexts that bestow the status of *auteur*. As Janet Staiger argues in an essay on Van Sant and authorship, "By conceptualizing authoring as a technique of the self, as a citational practice, an individual person 'authors' by duplicating recipes and exercises of authorship within a cultural and institutional context that understands such acts as signs of individuality."[12] Van Sant's films, Staiger contends, exemplify authorship as just such a citational practice, a critical procedure that retroactively selects out instances of stylistic repetition across a body of work. Van Sant playfully exploits this procedure throughout his films, as if anticipating the critical response. Staiger goes on to note:

> After the rise of *auteurism*, any art-school trained film director also knows that throwing in references to other works or one's own texts is part of creating an authorial signature (repetition creates the signature) and is part of the requirements necessary for the author-function to work.[13]

Similarly, Schneider has succinctly identified a number of these elements in Van Sant's work: themes of alienated youth, the iconography of the American West, nondiegetic inserts to represent heightened emotional experience, and time-lapse images of clouds. The *Psycho* remake includes these stylistic elements as well, including the nondiegetic inserts during both murders, the clouds behind the Bates home, and the added line of dialogue by the police officer ("Have a nice day"), which recalls the closing intertitle of *Private Idaho*. In both instances, Van Sant intends an ironic reading, as his characters are headed toward anything but a nice day.

It is these additions that Adrian Martin called Van Sant's "vague doodling in the margins."[14] Contrary to the critical impulse to separate Hitchcock from Van Sant, the master from his imitator—which is what one does when locating Van Sant's authorship only within his additions and deviations, important as they are, from Hitchcock's text, isolating his contributions to the film so as to value Hitchcock's more—Van Sant the author is to be found rather in both places, in the differences and imitations. Van Sant makes his deviations from the original no less imitative than the re-created shots. Again and again, images or camera movements or narrative structures—such as the inserts or "have a nice day"—are revealed to be reiterations of earlier texts, thereby derailing any process of attribution, as once one tries to attribute an authorial gesture to Van Sant, one is led to some anterior point even if that is his own earlier work. Though Martin claims that "by adopting the madness of the 'shot-by-shot remake,' Van Sant has denied himself the flexibility—even the very possibility—of arriving at his own *mise-en-scène*," nothing seems more antithetical to Van Sant's interests.[15] The *Psycho* remake demonstrates how Van Sant absents his own directorial presence by dissolving it into Hitchcock's own, asserting the mark of his authorship on the basis of its erasure.

Van Sant, looking to erase his own authorial presence, cloaking his identity in someone else's, selects a narrative of transvestism. Just as with Norman, who by the film's end becomes "all mother," her voice ventriloquizing his body, so too does Van Sant offer up his body—that is, the body of his film—so that Hitchcock may speak through it. The split personality of the spectator's viewing position is matched, then, in a splitting of the author, which makes Hitchcock and Van Sant both different and the same, or put differently, one body (i.e., the *Pyscho* text) which contains two voices. He both is and is not Hitchcock, and the original identity of Hitchcock the master, which critics would strive to locate within the remake, is thus occupied and confounded by the imitator. The transvestism of Hitchcock's film, though, is also a doubling (hence all the doubling of characters in mirrors) and Van Sant's film playfully exploits this. His cameo in the film occurs in the same place as Hitchcock's own, outside the real estate office, but this time he is shown talking to an actor dressed as the famed director, an image that both figuratively captures how the remake is a "conversation" of sorts between the two directors and visually indicates the film's schizophrenic divide between two directorial authorities.

Finally, the heresy of Van Sant's remake is that it strips away the central tenet of auteurist approaches to film studies: that an auteur is defined by his ability to put his own individual stamp on a film in the face of the constraints and limitations of industrial production. Auteurism is the triumph of art over commerce. Van Sant's film disrupts the very critical procedures of auteurism by which his film has been negatively judged—on the one hand, because his use of appropriation and imitation negates the original and individual stamp of the auteur, and on the other hand, because his remake confounds the distinction between commerce and art. Can the remake be considered a continuation of Warhol's notion of "business art," whereby the brand of the author denominates authorship regardless of the artist's actual contribution to the creation of the work? At the very least, Warhol's influence on Van Sant is most strongly felt in the upending of the distinction in value between art and commerce. Just as Warhol forced an encounter with the commodity image as an aesthetic object, Van Sant provides the reversed mirror image of that gesture, laying bare the commercial imperatives beneath the creation of the aesthetic object.

Ultimately, the innovation of Van Sant's shot-by-shot remake is that it challenges the very criteria by which remakes are evaluated and auteurism discriminated, but does so by embodying the practice in the most literal fashion possible: by reduplicating the object exactly and by self-consciously cultivating the citational practice that constitutes the mark of the author. The splitting of both the spectatorial response and of authorship find their origin in Hitchcock's film, as Norman's split personality structures and conditions the reception of the remake. The shot-by-shot remake is thus faithful to the original not simply because it is a re-creation but because that re-creation itself repeats the thematic content of Hitchcock's film. To criticize Van Sant's remake for not being sufficiently different from Hitchcock's film, or for merely "doodling in the margins," is to misjudge his project: to dismantle the myth of originality that underwrites critical approaches to film. Van Sant constructs his own authorial presence at the site of its disappearance, and following the model of Warhol, he recasts originality as imitation and appropriation.

Notes

The author wishes to thank the editors of *Hitchcock Annual* for their insightful comments on several drafts of my essay.

1. For a full account of the remake of *Pépé le Moko*, see Lucy Mazdon, "The Remake in History," in *Encore Hollywood: Remaking French Cinema* (London: British Film Institute Publishing, 2000), 30-50.

2. Paula Marantz Cohen, "The Artist Pays Homage," *Hitchcock Annual* 10 (2001-02): 128, 132.

3. Constantine Verevis, "*Psycho* (Redux)," *Hitchcock Annual* 10 (2001-02): 155-58.

4. Thomas Leitch, "Hitchcock Without Hitchcock," *Literature/Film Quarterly* 31, no. 4 (2003), 256.

5. Thomas Leitch, "Hitchcock without Hitchcock,", 257-58.

6. Patricia White, "On Retrospectatorship," in *Uninvited: Classical Hollywood Cinema and Lesbian Representability* (Bloomington: Indiana University Press, 1999), 194-215.

7. Thomas Leitch, "101 Ways to Tell Hitchcock's *Psycho* from Gus Van Sant's," *Literature/Film Quarterly* 31, no. 4 (2003): 269-73.

8. Esther Anatolitis, "Re-making the Remake: Gus Van Sant's *Psycho*," quoted in Steven Jay Schneider, "Van Sant the Provoca(u)teur," *Hitchcock Annual* 10 (2001-02), 141.

9. Quoted in Amy Taubin, "Objects of Desire," in *American Independent Cinema: A Sight and Sound Reader*, ed. Jim Hillier (London: BFI, 2001), 79-86, cited at 80.

10. Quoted in Janet Staiger, "Authorship Studies and Gus Van Sant," *Film Criticism* 29, no. 1 (2004), 11.

11. Schneider, "Van Sant the Provoca(u)teur."

12. Staiger, "Authorship Studies and Gus Van Sant," 2.

13. Staiger, "Authorship Studies and Gus Van Sant," 12.

14. Martin, "Shot-by-Shot Follies," *Hitchcock Annual* 10 (2001-02), 134.

15. Martin, "Shot-by-Shot Follies," 137.

Hitchcock, Unreliable Narration, and the Stalker Film

Alfred Hitchcock's influence on the horror genre since the 1960s has been widely acknowledged. Some scholars have pointed to the debt owed to Hitchcock's work by recent horror films such as *Halloween* (1978) and *Silence of the Lambs* (1991).[1] Others have suggested that his horror films *Psycho* (1960), and to a lesser extent *Frenzy* (1972), were responsible for shaping, if not initiating, larger trends in contemporary horror.[2] Most significantly for my purposes, Andrew Tudor has argued that *Psycho* helped inaugurate the shift from "security" to the "paranoia" that he sees as the hallmark of the genre since the 1960s. In secure horror, which prevailed in the genre's first four decades (1920-1960),

> the powers of disorder are always defeated by expertise and coercion, the genre world's authorities— whether those of science or of the state—remaining credible protectors of individual and social order. . . . The threat itself is likely to be external [to ordinary human society] than internal, and distant rather than proximate.[3]

But with the appearance of *Psycho* as well as Michael Powell's *Peeping Tom* (also 1960), things began to change. In part, these films were influential, claims Tudor, because they helped establish the psychotic trend in contemporary horror.[4] More important, their monsters, Norman and Mark, are ostensibly normal and live within human society, deceiving those around them. The clear distinction between ordinary humans and the abnormal monster who inhabits a remote location found in secure horror therefore breaks down, giving rise to paranoid horror. As Tudor points out, "However 'normal' friends, neighbors and family may seem, the presumption of paranoid horror is that they might prove unpredictably malevolent and so powerful that resistance is doomed to failure."[5]

Halloween and the cycle of stalker films its considerable commercial success helped initiate take this paranoia one step further, according to Tudor. Unlike Norman and Mark, *Halloween's* psychotic monster Michael Myers is "uncharacterized," and the film displays little interest in his psychology. Indeed, it is not clear he has one. Supposedly a normal boy living an ordinary existence in suburbia before the start of the film, he suddenly starts killing for no apparent reason. The film instead focuses almost entirely on the "terrorizing process" in which he hunts his victims, and the only questions raised are who, where, when, and how will he kill next. For Tudor, this is an even more paranoid form of horror than *Psycho* and *Peeping Tom's* because Michael's insanity "is no longer subject to reason, either as understanding or control," as was Norman and Mark's.[6] Nor can it be cured or stopped: Michael remains impervious to the therapeutic efforts of his psychiatrist, Dr. Loomis, and is able to survive all manner of physical injury to reappear in sequels.

A lack of security and monstrous humans who appear normal, even attractive, on the surface are prevalent in Hitchcock's work in general, not just *Psycho*. As Maurice Yacowar puts it, Hitchcock's "world is full of uncertainty" and his films "refuse the confidence of a secure order."[7] Nor is this insecurity confined to the characters, according to Yacowar, for Hitchcock "exploits the insecurity of his audience." Yacowar also points to the way he does this: by "continually violat[ing] his viewer's expectations."[8] This violation, I argue here, is achieved in part by way of a distinctive brand of unreliable narration, which I will delineate. Then, rather than focusing on the influence of *Psycho's* characters and themes on contemporary horror, as Tudor and others have, I examine how *Halloween* and other stalker films both employ and extend Hitchcock's type of unreliable narration, sometimes in ingenious ways. I argue that it is not just the characters in these films who cannot be trusted, but the narration itself, which plays a large role in creating the viewer's insecurity that is definitive both of Hitchcock's films and, according to Tudor, contemporary horror.

I

The standard definition of unreliable narration is Wayne Booth's, according to which a narrator is "*reliable* when he speaks for or acts in accordance with the norms of the work (which is to say, the implied author's norms), *unreliable* when he does not."[9] When reading an unreliable narrative, the reader is supposed to notice a discrepancy between the intentions of the author as implied by the work and the narrator's story. Bret Easton Ellis's novel *American Psycho* (1991), for example, is a first-person narrative in which the character-narrator, Patrick Bateman, tells of his daily life as a wealthy investment banker and serial killer in Manhattan. As the events he narrates become more and more improbable, the reader begins to ask whether the implied author intends him or her to infer that these events are not really happening and that Bateman is delusional, a question that is never definitively answered. Hitchcock, of course, is famous for experimenting with a similar kind of unreliable narration in *Stage Fright* (1950), in which a character, Johnny, tells another character how he discovered the victim of a murder of which he has been wrongly accused, which is narrated by what appears to be a flashback. However, at the end of the film, we learn that this story was a lie, that Johnny is the murderer, and that the flashback was not objectively accurate.[10]

There are important differences between these two examples, but in both the viewer is initially misled, assuming at first that the narration of a character is reliable, only to discover later that it is not.[11] Unreliable narration need not be deceptive, however. The viewer of *Rashomon* (1950) has no reason initially to distrust the accounts of the woodcutter, the priest, and the bandit Tajomaru about their involvement in the case of the dead samurai and his wife. But once the woodcutter explicitly repudiates Tajomaru's version of events and begins a philosophical discussion with the commoner and the priest about the human propensity for lying and self-deception, the viewer distrusts the stories subsequently told by the wife, the dead husband, and the woodcutter himself, a distrust that intensifies due to the incompatibilities between them as well as the earlier reports. In the case of these three character-narrators, we do not initially assume that their accounts are reliable only to learn retrospectively that they were not and we were deceived, as in *American Psycho* and *Stage Fright*. Instead, we are aware of their possible unreliability as they are told and are therefore not mislead. Similarly, the viewer of *Last Year at Marienbad* (1961) quickly becomes cognizant of the disagreements between the characters about events in the past and the fact that various versions of these events will be shown. Again, the viewer is not deceived into believing that one of these versions is true only to learn later that it is not. Rather, we are aware from early on in the film that they are all potentially unreliable.

Some narratologists, such as Seymour Chatman, have argued that the concept of unreliable narration should be restricted to examples such as these, in which there is "some clearly discernible discrepancy between the narrator's account and the larger implied meaning of the narrative as a whole."[12] Indeed, Chatman believes that genuine examples of unreliable narration are few and far between in film "because, perhaps, the viewing public is not as ready for narrative ironies as is the reading public."[13] David Bordwell, however, has suggested that a different kind of unreliable narration can be found in Hitchcock's work. In the *Stage Fright* example, the flashback is unreliable in the sense of not being truthful. But the term unreliable can also refer to the narration's communicativeness, Bordwell argues. Hitchcock's narration, he points out, at certain moments "withholds information to

Figure 1

which its degree of knowledge entitles it . . . exactly the sort of information to which it has earlier claimed complete access." Furthermore, it does so in a manner that draws attention to itself, thereby flaunting its capacity to control what the viewer knows and when.[14] Although this is in part a transtextual norm of the thriller, the genre in which Hitchcock usually worked, Hitchcock takes it much further. His narration cannot always be relied on to give the viewer information it has access to and has previously provided, and the viewer begins to distrust it.[15]

This type of unreliable narration, which I will call unreliably communicative narration, is far more common in Hitchcock's films than the well-known example of the objectively inaccurate flashback in *Stage Fright*. *Frenzy* provides a canonical example. After an omniscient opening helicopter shot of London, which ends on a dissolve to a gathering by the Thames where one of the Necktie Murderer's victims is discovered, the narration is largely restricted to Richard Blaney's knowledge until Bob Rusk goes to see Brenda Blaney in her office. Having told her that she is his "type of woman," he brutally rapes and murders her, and the narration is infamously communicative, allowing the viewer to witness much of the horrific crime. But when Babs Milligan goes with Rusk to his flat later in the film, the camera, having accompanied her and Rusk up the stairs to the door of the flat, unexpectedly reverses direction just as he tells her that she is his "kind of woman" (fig. 1). The camera descends the stairs and

Figure 2

onto the street in a virtuoso travelling shot, finally coming to rest on a long shot of the building in front of which passersby go about their daily activities, oblivious to the crime that is probably taking place inside (fig. 2). It is not just that we have had previously unrestricted access to a similar event that foregrounds the narration's refusal to grant it to us here. It is also the choice of stylistic technique, a camera movement that teases us into assuming we will be privy to what transpires between Rusk and Babs, only to prolong our disappointment (or relief) through its slow backward motion which, in its independence from character movement, is highly overt.

This example illustrates the two major criteria of unreliably communicative narration: the narration's unpredictable departure from previously established norms of knowledge and communicativeness, and the explicitness with which this is done. It shows that unreliable communication is context-bound, only standing out relative to a narration's communicative norm. All narration is uncommunicative to a greater or lesser extent. Typically, however, as Bordwell has suggested, a film's narration establishes a norm of communicativeness to which it largely adheres, and deviations from this norm can usually be motivated generically. The narration of detective films, for example, is often restricted to the range of knowledge of the detective. But it is also a convention of the detective film that "the narration can inject hints, clues and false leads which the detective does not recognize."[16] What distinguishes Hitchcock's

Figure 3

narration is that its departures from its own communicative norms are conspicuous and cannot always be motivated generically. They therefore have to be justified authorially as a distinct characteristic of his films.

Unlike many detective, serial killer, and horror films, for example, *Frenzy*'s narration deviates from the communicative norm of restricting the range of knowledge to the "wrong man," Richard Blaney, in order to reveal the identity of the killer early in the film rather than waiting until the end, and there is therefore no generic reason why it hides Rusk's murder of Babs in such a flamboyant manner. Similarly, *Vertigo* (1958) establishes the communicative norm of restricting its range of knowledge almost entirely to what retired detective Scottie Ferguson knows. However, two-thirds of the way through the film, after Scottie has left Judy Barton in her hotel room for the first time, the narration suddenly reveals what he does not know: that Judy did in fact pretend to be Gavin Elster's now-deceased wife, Madeleine, with whom he was in love, and that together they deceived Scottie into believing that Madeleine died at the San Juan Bautista mission. Once again this departure from the narration's communicative norm cannot be motivated generically, as it is a convention of the detective and mystery film to reveal the truth at the end. And yet again it occurs in a highly self-conscious manner. After Scottie leaves the hotel room, the camera pans left to a close-up of Judy (fig. 3). She stares directly into it, her face twisted in distress, as the image turns red and a flashback begins, which reveals the deception perpetrated on Scottie at the mission. Rather than withholding information previously provided, as in the example from *Frenzy*, the narration here does the opposite: revealing what was previously concealed. But in both, the narration explicitly deviates from the communicative norm it has established in ways that cannot be motivated generically.

Unreliably communicative narration is not necessarily deceptive. It is unreliable not because it imparts seemingly reliable but ultimately false information that leads the viewer to make the wrong inferences, as in *Stage Fright* and *American Psycho*, but because the access it gives to true information varies unpredictably and noticeably. There are, however, two variants of unreliably communicative narration in Hitchcock's work that do involve misleading the viewer. An example of the first—call it deceptively uncommunicative narration— occurs in the suspenseful scene in *Marnie* (1964) in which the eponymous heroine robs Rutland and Co. Until this moment, although the narration has been largely restricted to Marnie's knowledge, it has exhibited moments of omniscience as in *Frenzy*: the cut at the beginning from a woman we will soon discover is Marnie escaping from a robbery by train to Mr. Strutt, the victim of that robbery, reporting it to the police in his office; and again when the associate of one of Marnie's previous victims observes her and Mark Rutland at a race track unbeknownst to them. While Marnie is robbing the safe in Mark's firm after the other office workers have departed for the evening, a long shot reveals a cleaning woman mopping the floor in an adjacent corridor (fig. 4).[17] Having discovered her presence, Marnie takes off her shoes, puts one in each of her coat pockets, and tip-toes toward the stairs in an effort to escape undetected. Hitchcock cuts from shots of Marnie's head and feet as she passes the cleaning woman to shots of one of the shoes gradually slipping out of her pocket, something Marnie is unaware of. Finally, it falls to the ground, making a loud sound. Marnie, suspecting she has been discovered, turns to look back at the woman who, inexplicably, continues mopping, oblivious to her presence.

Figure 4

As she picks up the shoe and finally escapes down the stairs, a man appears and shouts a greeting in the cleaning woman's ear, revealing her to be hard of hearing.

In this variant of unreliably communicative narration, rather than advertising the fact that it is being uncommunicative, as in the example of Babs's murder in *Frenzy*, the narration at first hides it, concealing the cleaning woman's hearing impairment and tricking the viewer into assuming like Marnie that if she makes a sound she will be discovered, thereby generating suspense. Only retroactively, once the truth is revealed, do we realize that we were not in possession of all the relevant facts, and that if we had been, we would not have felt so much anxious uncertainty for Marnie. The moments of unrestricted narration in which the viewer knows more than Marnie—the initial appearance of the cleaning woman, the shots of the slipping shoe, the revelation of the cleaning woman's hearing problem—only serve to demonstrate, along with the omniscient narration earlier in the film, that the narration could have been more forthcoming. From now on, we know that we cannot trust the narration to reveal everything it could and that our subsequent emotional reactions might be premised on incomplete information.

In addition to hiding the fact that it is being uncommunicative, Hitchcock's narration sometimes creates the appearance of being communicative only to reveal later that it has misled the viewer. As Richard Allen has shown in meticulous detail, Hitchcock films Ivor Novello in *The Lodger* (1927) using expressionist techniques commonly employed to depict monsters and other evil characters in expressionist films of the 1920s, thereby implying that his character, the lodger, is the serial killer who is preying upon young blonde women in London. In fact, he turns out to be the brother of one of the murdered women who seeks to avenge her death. As Allen aptly describes it, when the lodger first appears at the Buntings' door, his "phantom-like presence emerging out of the London fog resembles *Nosferatu* and . . . Mrs. Bunting's reaction recalls the astonishment of the heroine of *The Cabinet of Dr. Caligari* when Caligari as showman reveals to her the rigid body of the phallic somnambulist lying down in the coffin-like 'cabinet.' "[18] In this variant—which can be termed deceptively communicative narration—seemingly communicative stylistic and other narrational cues encourage the viewer to make inferences and assumptions that later turn out to be false.

Hitchcock's use of unreliably communicative narration, especially the two deceptive varieties I have just described, is one of the reasons he is often viewed as a "manipulative" filmmaker who "plays" an interactive "game" with his viewers in an effort to outwit them, an idea most fully explored by Thomas Leitch. According to Leitch, the game of spotting Hitchcock's cameo appearances in his films is emblematic of the director's larger "conception of narration as a game between a storyteller and an audience" in which the filmmaker plays hide and seek with the truth, which the viewer tries to discern.[19] What is particularly distinctive about the way Hitchcock plays this game, according to Leitch, is the way he "keeps changing the rules."[20] For example, in his films of the mid-1930s, particularly the first version of *The Man Who Knew Too Much* (1934), Hitchcock encourages "the audience to adopt the wrong expectations and so to misread the tone of particular scenes and the film as a whole," switching from "grave to gay" unpredictably and misleadingly.[21] When Bob Lawrence and Uncle Clive visit a sinister dentist in Wapping in an effort to find Bob's kidnapped daughter, for instance, Bob waits outside in the reception area while Clive, pretending to have a toothache, goes inside. When Bob hears Clive scream, he draws his pistol, only to discover that the dentist has merely pulled Clive's tooth. This is an example of what I have been calling deceptively communicative narration, for as in *The Lodger*, the viewer is led to make a false inference by misleading narrational cues, and in general what Leitch refers to as Hitchcock's penchant for "changing the rules" can be explained by unreliably communicative narration.

Interestingly, at least one scholar of contemporary horror has described the stalker film as an interactive game. Just as Hitchcock's viewers must try to spot his appearances, so the viewer of *Halloween* and other stalker films must try and guess where, when, who, and how the monster will kill next. Watching a stalker film is therefore like "playing a video game" in which one participates, Vera Dika has argued, in part because stalker films employ narrational cues to keep the viewer guessing the monster's whereabouts:

> Here the killer's position is assessed by a number of cues, carried out primarily by the type of shot or the sequence of shots. By these conventionalized indicators of the killer's presence, the audience is given a knowledge of his murderous threat before the film's characters have become aware of it. These techniques create the film's suspense but, also, the film's game. The fact that these cues are not always truthful or "effective" (i.e., the killer may be in the victim's space but choose not to attack) gives the viewer the opportunity to "warn" the victims, while it also encourages a play with the film's authorial system. In this way, the formal manipulations are used to shock the spectator in the stalker film but also to encourage his/her involvement in the game.[22]

Dika does not analyze these "formal manipulations" in detail. But, as we will see, they consist primarily of the distinctive kind of unreliable narration we find in Hitchcock's films, which *Halloween*, a film that self-consciously alludes to *Psycho* and was made by a director who grew up watching Hitchcock's films, introduced to the stalker film.

II

Halloween's debt to *Psycho* is overtly acknowledged by the film in multiple ways, from the empty eye sockets in the Halloween pumpkin during the credit sequence, which echo the empty eye sockets of *Psycho*'s skull motif, to Dr. Loomis, who shares the same last name with Sam, one of *Psycho*'s characters.[23] Its opening scene, which takes place in suburban Haddonfield, Illinois, on Halloween night in 1963, just as self-consciously signals its inheritance of Hitchcock's brand of unreliable narration by departing from a convention that *Psycho* helped to set in place. The scene consists almost entirely of a single point-of-view shot from the perspective of someone outside a house spying on a couple kissing inside, who then enters, grabs a knife, waits for the woman's boyfriend to leave, and climbs the stairs to her bedroom, where he puts on a mask and stabs her. As she fends of the attacker, she screams his name, "Michael," and falls to the floor covered in blood. The point-of-view shot continues as the stalker moves downstairs and out of the house just as a car pulls up outside. The occupants approach Michael, say his name, and begin to lift off his mask. There is a cut to a crane shot that pulls away from the attacker who is revealed to be a young boy in a Halloween costume, and the scene ends.

As Steve Neale was the first to observe, the point-of-view shot in this scene creates a hierarchy of knowledge in which the viewer knows more than the characters being stalked but does not know everything, principally the identity of the stalker.[24] It informs the viewer that someone is watching and following the young man and woman in the house unbeknownst to them, without identifying that person. Even after he is named, the revelation that he is a child is a surprise, given the absence of child psychotics in horror films prior to this time. The unusual length of the point-of-view shot (4 minutes, 7 seconds), which departs from the norm of quickly identifying the source of point-of-view shots, advertises the narration's capacity to withhold information, in this case the identity of the stalker. So does the omniscient crane shot, which the narration could have supplied earlier. Yet, when that second shot reveals the attacker to be a child, we realize that the point-of-view shot not only overtly hid the identity of the stalker, but covertly disguised the fact that he is a child, thereby departing from the convention of the adult male psychotic established by *Psycho* and *Peeping Tom*. Right from its opening scene, therefore, *Halloween* announces that its narration may be deceptively uncommunicative, concealing the fact that it is hiding information, in this case that the killer is a child, and thereby leading the viewer to make false inferences.

Fifteen years later, Michael escapes from the psychiatric hospital where he has been incarcerated since the murder of the young woman, who turns out to have been his sister, Judith. The next day, which is Halloween, Dr. Loomis travels several hundred miles from the hospital to Haddonfield in an attempt to warn the local authorities that Michael may be returning to murder again. Meanwhile, Michael, who has indeed gone back to Haddonfield, begins to stalk Laurie Strode and her friends Annie, Lynda, and Tommy. It is now that the narration begins playing the guessing game with the viewer about who, when, where, and how Michael will kill. It does this by revealing that Michael is near one or more of the young people, but concealing precisely where he is, thereby forcing the viewer to scan the space around the characters in an attempt to locate him. A good example occurs when Michael is stalking Annie, who will become his first contemporary victim in Haddonfield. Annie is talking on the phone to her boyfriend in the kitchen of the house where she is babysitting Lindsay Wallace, her back to the garden door. The camera pans to keep her in the center of the frame as she moves from left to right, with the door onscreen one moment, off-screen the next. As it comes back on-screen during one pan, one of Carpenter's stingers—a musical cue consisting of a sound made on a synthesizer—alerts the viewer to Michael's presence just outside it, looking at Annie. Unawares, she moves again to the left and, as before, the camera pans to follow her, the door and Michael moving off-screen. When she moves back and the door once again becomes visible, Michael is gone. This narrational game in which Michael is revealed one moment and concealed the next continues until the final confrontation between Michael and Laurie at the end of the film, and it quickly becomes the film's communicative norm. Indeed, due to the success of the film, it became a transtextual convention of the stalker sub-genre. However, similar to what Leitch observed in many of Hitchcock's films, the narration in *Halloween* keeps "changing the rules" of the game by departing from this communicative norm explicitly and unpredictably as the film progresses.

The most obvious example involves the point-of-view shot introduced in the opening scene. When we first see Laurie in Haddonfield on her way to school on Halloween day 1978, her father, a real estate agent, asks her to drop off a key at the Myers house, which stands derelict and uninhabited. She is joined by young Tommy, whom she will babysit that night. As they reach the house, we cut to a long shot of them from inside the house through the window of the front door, which Laurie approaches (fig. 5). On the soundtrack, the heavy breathing that we heard in the opening scene after Michael put on his Halloween mask begins, suggesting that he is nearby. After several brief exterior shots as Laurie bends down to slide the key under the door, we cut back to the long shot through the door window and Michael suddenly steps into the frame from the right, his appearance accompanied by a stinger (fig. 6). His back to the camera, he looks through the window at Laurie as she slides the key under the door and goes back down the garden path to join Tommy, thereby turning the shot into an approximate point-of-view shot from his perspective. Moments later this new norm is repeated after Tommy has left Laurie and she walks away from the Myers house (fig. 7). Again, Michael steps into the right-hand side of the frame, turning the shot into a rough point-of-view (fig. 8).

Figure 5

Figure 6

Figure 7

Figure 8

By using this technique, Carpenter both invokes and departs from the communicative norm established by the point-of-view shot in the opening scene. Like that shot, these point-of-view shots are communicative, creating a hierarchy of knowledge in which the viewer knows that Michael is watching one or more characters who are oblivious to his presence. However, unlike that shot, both are at first deceptively uncommunicative, hiding the fact that they will become point-of-view shots from Michael's approximate perspective and thereby generating surprise when he moves into the frame. A technique that was partially communicative in the first scene, revealing Michael's presence but hiding his identity, is therefore turned into one that is initially uncommunicative about his whereabouts. But that is not all. These two point-of-view shots prime the viewer to expect that any long shot might turn into a point-of-view shot from Michael's perspective, and from then on when we see one we look at the corner of the frame, anticipating that Michael might step into it. Shortly afterward at the local school, he does—but this time from the left rather than the right. Now we have to pay attention to both the left and the right sides of the frame. In a further twist, after Michael has driven past Laurie and her friends on their way home from school, the narration holds on a long shot of them as they walk down the street, much as it did when Laurie left the Myers house. The shot is unbalanced, with an empty space on the left, suggesting Michael might step into the frame as before (fig. 9). He doesn't, however, and the viewer is left wondering whether he is nearby. From now on, we never know whether a long shot is a potential point-of-view from Michael's perspective, and it therefore becomes a highly unreliable technique.

The narration plays a similar game with another stylistic cue. From the very beginning of the film, Michael tends to watch his victims through windows and doors before attacking them, and the viewer learns to pay attention to any aperture in a scene to see if Michael is lurking in it. After Laurie has discovered her dead friends, for example, she cowers near a dark doorway, terrified and sobbing. The audience scans it for

Figure 9

any signs of him, and sure enough, he slowly emerges, his presence again signaled by a stinger. Much like point-of-view shots, apertures are therefore a partially communicative stylistic cue, informing the viewer of Michael's whereabouts. However, again like the point-of-view shots, they are unreliably communicative. Sometimes Michael is not present in a dark aperture; at other times there are multiple dark apertures in a space, any one of which might conceal his presence; and often he does not attack even when he is revealed to be in an aperture. The laundry room that Annie visits shortly before her death is a good example, for it contains three apertures: the door to the room, a window, and a dark doorway in the room.

When Annie first enters, the viewer looks back and forth between all three to see if Michael is hiding in one (figs. 10 and 11). Michael soon appears, watching Annie through the door (fig. 12), but disappears again when she senses his presence and goes to investigate, only to reappear in the window behind her after the door becomes jammed and she shouts for help (fig. 13). Annie then gets stuck trying to climb out of the window that Michael has just appeared in, but he does not strike, and Lindsay, her charge, arrives to let her out. In this scene, the third aperture, the dark doorway in the laundry room, remains empty, signaling that dark apertures do not always conceal Michael, and Michael does not attack from the two others in which he does appear, the doorway and the window, even though Annie sticks her head into both. Apertures are therefore rendered unreliably communicative, sometimes signaling Michael's presence, sometimes not.

Figure 10

Figure 11

Figure 12

Figure 13

Even the hierarchy of knowledge that is a norm through much of the film ultimately proves to be unreliable. Walking home from school with Annie, Laurie sees Michael watching them from behind a hedge in front of Annie's house, although at this point she does not know who he is. After investigating and finding nothing behind the hedge, Annie goes into her house, while Laurie walks on, looking back at the hedge in a close-up shot. After a brief point-of-view shot of the hedge from her perspective, we cut back again to the close-up of her when, suddenly, an unidentified man appears in the right of the frame, whom she bumps into. Momentarily startled like the viewer, she screams, but a reverse angle reveals the man to be Annie's father, a local police officer, rather than Michael. Here, by way of the close-up, the narration hides the police officer's proximity. Furthermore, his dark canvas police jacket is similar to the dark overalls Michael is wearing, and, with his back to the camera, it is easy to mistake him for Michael, especially as we know Michael is nearby. Something similar happens when Annie brings Lindsay across the street to the house where Laurie is babysitting Tommy. That Annie and Lindsay are leaving the house where Michael has been lurking lulls the viewer into a false sense of security. But after they cross the road, Michael suddenly stands up from behind a car where he has been hiding. This motion is accompanied by a loud stinger, startling the audience. The narration, in other words, cannot always be trusted to reveal whether Michael is nearby, thereby generating surprise when he emerges unexpectedly into the frame, and it sometimes tricks the viewer into confusing other characters with him through deceptive cues such as the police officer's jacket—much like Hitchcock confuses the viewer about the identity of the lodger.

Halloween's employment of unreliably communicative narration, and the insecurity it creates, is self-consciously acknowledged by its coda. After Dr. Loomis has shot Michael multiple times only to discover that he has disappeared again, he stares worriedly into the distance while Laurie begins to cry. Carpenter's now-famous musical score begins, and the narration cuts to shots of empty spaces that Michael has previously inhabited, ending on the derelict Myers house. In part, as Tudor has pointed out, this serves to emphasize the monstrous threat that continues to lurk somewhere among the "prosaic" streets and houses of Haddonfield, thereby rendering suburbia, normally associated with security, unsafe.[25] But in addition, it reprises and sums up the central narrational conceit of the film: omnisciently communicating that Michael is nearby and simultaneously concealing precisely where he is in part by establishing communicative norms which are then overtly and unexpectedly departed from. Prior to the coda, the sound of Michael's breathing has been a reliable cue that he is nearby. But in the coda itself, this cue accompanies all of the shots of the empty spaces, suggesting that he might be in any one of them. Like the point-of-view shots, apertures, and hierarchy of knowledge norms, in other words, it has become unreliably communicative.

III

Few of the stalker films that followed *Halloween* proved to be as innovative in their use of Hitchcock's brand of unreliable narration, and most simply copied the techniques pioneered by Carpenter. *Halloween II* (1981), which Carpenter produced and co-wrote but did not direct, takes place immediately after the events in *Halloween*. Michael is on the loose having survived, seemingly uninjured, the attempts by Laurie and Dr. Loomis to kill him. As he roams the neighborhood, he kills various people he comes across. In one scene, a young woman is talking on the phone to a friend about the killings that have taken place that night. After a shot of Michael looking at her through the window of her house, we cut inside to a close-up of the woman, who has her back to a door to the house, much like Annie in *Halloween*. Michael slips in through the door, and moves off-screen, making a sound in the process. Startled, she turns around and nervously goes to investigate, pausing to ask "Who is it?" As in the earlier film, the viewer scans the space around her, trying to determine where Michael will attack from. Suddenly, accompanied by a stinger, he leaps up from beneath the camera and cuts her throat. While the narration is successful at generating suspense and drawing the viewer into the guessing game about Michael's whereabouts, it hardly breaks new ground here, relying on the techniques—hierarchy of knowledge and apertures—already familiar from the earlier film.

Nevertheless, a few stalker films managed to be more innovative in their use of unreliably communicative narration. A good example is *Friday 13th Part 2* (1981), in which a stalker spies on and then kills one by one a group of counselors gathered at a summer training camp. From the beginning, the narration employs point-of-view shots from the perspective of an unidentified observer, as in *Halloween*. However, it finds a way to render such shots even more unreliable than Carpenter's. In the opening scene, Alice, the survivor of the first *Friday 13th* (1980), restlessly wanders around her apartment, the camera following her. Shots of the feet of an unidentified person outside her building, along with ominous music on the soundtrack, have already alerted us to the possible presence of a stalker. Eventually, Alice takes a shower, the camera waiting outside her bathroom in the hallway. Slowly, it begins to advance down the hall, turns the corner into the bathroom, and approaches the shower. The fact that it is moving independently of any character is a powerful cue that it is a point-of-view shot. However, Alice opens the shower curtain and we cut to a new shot—it turns out that we have been tricked and the moving shot was not a point-of-view shot at all. Rather than rendering certain shots unreliable by making the viewer unsure whether they will become point-of-view shots from the killer's position, as in *Halloween*, the filmmakers here use deceptively communicative narration, in which a misleading cue—a camera moving independently of characters—leads the viewer to misidentify a shot as a point-of-view shot.

The narration continues to play with this technique of false point-of-views in ingenious ways. Later at the camp, a counselor, Vicky, prepares for a rendezvous with another counselor, who is in a wheelchair. She leaves her cabin to fetch something from her car, and bends down inside. The camera begins to slowly approach her from behind, accompanied by ominous music, once again suggesting that it might represent a stalker's point-of-view. But it turns out to be a false alarm when Vicky closes the car door and continues about her business. Immediately afterward, in a different cabin, her wheel-bound paramour thinks he hears her outside and wheels himself out to investigate (fig. 14). As he sits on the deck, the camera slowly approaches him from behind accompanied by the same music as before (fig. 15). As we have just seen a false point-of-view shot, we know this one might be too, something that appears to be confirmed by a reverse shot that reveals the space behind him to be empty. Again we cut back to the slowly approaching potential point-of-view shot, and again another reverse shot shows nothing behind him. We cut back behind him a third time, the camera closer to his head now, and suddenly a machete strikes his face from screen right (fig. 16) and he rolls back, screaming in agony. The point-of-view shot turns out to have been false once again—the stalker was not behind him. But unlike before, he was there all the same, approaching from a different direction. Here, the fake point-of-view shot is not only misleading, potentially leading the viewer to infer that the killer is behind his victim, but it helps conceal the position from which the killer actually does eventually strike, thereby combining deceptively uncommunicative narration with the deceptively communicative variety. Now that's unreliable!

III

Hitchcock's influence on contemporary horror is not confined to characters who hide their perverse, psychotic natures behind outwardly appealing facades, such as Norman Bates and Bob Rusk, as well as the insecure world they inhabit. Hitchcock also showed Carpenter and other directors of stalker films a way of making viewers experience insecurity with his distinct type of unreliable narration, which establishes

Figure 14

Figure 15

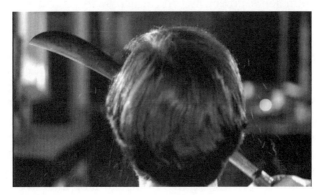

Figure 16

communicative norms only to depart from them unexpectedly and sometimes misleadingly. The resultant inability to trust the narration is one reason for the insecurity felt by the viewer of both Hitchcock's films and the stalker sub-genre. In Hitchcock's work, and I suspect in Carpenter's too, unreliable narration is part and parcel of the auteur's larger worldview, which emphasizes chaos, disorder, and the unpredictability of events. In many stalker films, however, it is simply a means to the end of creating an entertaining experience for viewers.[26]

This type of narration also reminds us that "unreliable" means "untrustworthy," and that there are a variety of reasons one can distrust someone. One reason, of course, is that the person lies, is mistaken, or is self-deluded, as in the cases of the character-narrators in *Stage Fright*, *Last Year at Marienbad*, and *Rashomon*. But people can also be untrustworthy because they are unreliable sources of information, telling us the truth sometimes while overtly withholding it at others. As Bordwell has astutely pointed out, it is in this sense that the narration in Hitchcock's films is often unreliable and, as I have shown, the same is the case with stalker films. Nor are these the only examples of unreliably communicative narration in the history of cinema. Miklós Jancsó's early films, for example, pan and track to reveal off-screen events at one moment, only to conceal them at the next seemingly for no reason except to make the viewer aware of the filmmaker's power to control access to information and thereby experience power in the hands of an arbitrary authority, just as the characters in his films do.

These examples demonstrate, as Gregory Currie has also argued, that there are other kinds of unreliable narration in film in addition to the type identified by Booth in which there is a discrepancy between the narrator's story and the larger meaning of the work.[27] Unreliable communication of the non-deceptive sort occurs when the narration self-consciously deviates from a communicative norm it has already established. The discrepancy is between the narration's own norm of communicativeness and its departures from that norm, not the narrator and the implied author's meaning. When it is deceptive, this is again due to discrepancies between different moments in the narration. While Booth has highlighted one important kind of unreliable narration, there are others too, including the unreliably communicative variety delineated here.

Notes

I thank Richard Allen and Sidney Gottlieb for their helpful comments on an earlier draft of this paper.

1. Vera Dika, *Games of Terror: Halloween, Friday the 13th, and the Films of the Stalker Cycle* (London: Associated University Presses, 1990), 33-52; Lesley Brill, "Hitchcockian *Silence*: *Psycho* and Jonathan Demme's *The Silence of the Lambs*," in *After Hitchcock: Influence, Imitation, and Intertextuality*, ed. David Boyd and R. Barton Palmer (Austin: University of Texas Press, 2006), 31-46.

2. On the legacy of *Frenzy*, see Adam Lowenstein, "The Master, the Maniac, and *Frenzy*: Hitchcock's Legacy of Horror," in *Hitchcock: Past and Future*, ed. Richard Allen and Sam Ishii-Gonzáles (London: Routledge, 2004), 179-92.

3. Andrew Tudor, *Monsters and Mad Scientists: A Cultural History of the Horror Movie* (Oxford: Blackwell, 1989), 214.

4. By the early 1980s, according to Tudor's statistics, the monster is a psychotic in over 50% of horror films.

5. Tudor, *Monsters and Mad Scientists*, 221.

6. Tudor, *Monsters and Mad Scientists*, 207.

7. Maurice Yacowar, "Hitchcock's Imagery and Art," in *A Hitchcock Reader*, ed. Marshall Deutelbaum and Leland Poague (Ames: Iowa State University Press, 1986), 17.

8. Yacowar, "Hitchcock's Imagery and Art," 20-21.

9. Wayne C. Booth, *The Rhetoric of Fiction*, second ed. (Chicago: University of Chicago Press, 1983), 158-59.

10. As Sidney Gottlieb has pointed out to me, Hitchcock experiments with something similar as early as *Champagne* (1928), in which we see the character of Betty being assaulted by "the Man," only to discover that this sequence portrays her fantasy rather than reality.

11. One important difference is that in *Stage Fright*, Johnny, the unreliable narrator, is not the fictional source of the images and sounds we perceive in the lying flashback, unlike Patrick Bateman who is, fictionally, the source of the words we read in *American Psycho*.

On the differences between unreliable narration in film and literature, see Gregory Currie, *Image and Mind: Film, Philosophy, and Cognitive Science* (Cambridge: University of Cambridge Press, 1995), 265-70.

12. Seymour Chatman, *Coming to Terms: The Rhetoric of Narrative in Fiction and Film* (Ithaca: Cornell University Press, 1990), 137.

13. Chatman, *Coming to Terms*, 131.

14. David Bordwell, *Narration in the Fiction Film* (London: Routledge, 1985), 59-60.

15. In this paper, I follow Bordwell in referring to "the narration" rather than "the narrator." However, unlike him, I remain undecided as to whether films have narrators (other than character narrators).

16. Bordwell, *Narration in the Fiction Film*, 59.

17. Here, Hitchcock, as was his wont, subverts classical suspense—in which two outcomes are possible, one of which is wished for but unlikely and moral, the other likely but undesirable and immoral—aligning the viewer with Marnie's immoral desire to rob the safe undetected by intensifying the anxious uncertainty we feel about her capacity to do so through a mixture of both omniscient and restricted narration. See Richard Allen's analysis of Hitchcockian suspense in chapter two of *Hitchcock's Romantic Irony* (New York: Columbia University Press, 2007).

18. Richard Allen, "*The Lodger* and the Origins of Hitchcock's Aesthetic," *Hitchcock Annual* (2001-2002), 58.

19. Thomas M. Leitch, *Find the Director and Other Hitchcock Games* (Athens: University of Georgia Press, 1991), 7.

20. Leitch, *Find the Director*, 17.

21. Leitch, *Find the Director*, 76-77.

22. Dika, *Games of Terror*, 22.

23. The debt to *Psycho* was recognized immediately by reviewers; see, for example, Tom Allen, "A Sleeper That's Here to Stay," *Village Voice*, November 6, 1978.

24. Steve Neale, "*Halloween*: Suspense, Aggression and the Look," *Framework* 14 (1981): 25-29.

25. Tudor, *Monsters and Mad Scientists*, 201.

26. I owe this suggestion to Richard Allen.

27. Currie claims to have found another kind of unreliable narration in film. Because he believes that all narrators in films are diegetically "embedded," it is possible that a character-narrator's story might be made unreliable by narrational cues that do not have their source in another character's story. To accommodate this possibility, he argues for a conception of unreliable narration different from Booth's in which the implied author is the source of the unreliability. See Currie, *Image and Mind*, 269-70.

Contributors

Sidney Gottlieb is Professor of Media Studies and Digital Culture at Sacred Heart University, Fairfield, Connecticut. He is working on a full-text version of the Hitchcock/Truffaut interview.

James MacDowell is completing a doctoral thesis at the University of Warwick on the subject of the Hollywood "happy ending." He is a member of the editorial board of *Movie: A Journal of Film Criticism*.

David Sterritt is chair of the National Society of Film Critics, chief book critic of *Film Quarterly*, film critic of *Tikkun*, and adjunct professor of film at Columbia University and the Maryland Institute College of Art. His books include *The Films of Alfred Hitchcock* (Cambridge University Press, 1993).

Malcolm Turvey teaches film studies at Sarah Lawrence College and is an editor of *October*. He is the author of *Doubting Vision: Film and the Revelationist Tradition* (Oxford University Press, 2008) and *The Filming of Modern Life: European Avant-Garde Film of the 1920s* (MIT Press, forthcoming).

Graig Uhlin is a Ph.D. candidate in Cinema Studies at New York University. He has articles on Andy Warhol forthcoming in *Cinema Journal* and *Quarterly Review of Film and Video*. He is currently at work on a dissertation on temporality in classical film theory and aesthetics.

James M. Vest is professor emeritus of French, Film Studies, and Interdisciplinary Humanities at Rhodes College. His writings include numerous articles on French authors, approaches to interdisciplinary teaching, Hitchcock, and Truffaut. His most recent book is *Hitchcock and France: The Forging of an Auteur*.

Michael Walker is a retired teacher who is on the editorial board of *Movie* magazine. He has contributed to *The Movie Book of Film Noir*, *The Movie Book of the Western*, and *Alfred Hitchcock: Centenary Essays*. His book *Hitchcock's Motifs* was published by Amsterdam University Press in 2005.